From Balfour to Oslo: The History of the Arab Israeli Conflict

Copyright Page

TITLE: From Balfour to Oslo: A History of the Arab-Israeli Conflict

1ST Edition

Copyright @ 2023

ISBN: 9798223681458

Table of Contents

From Balfour to Oslo: A History of the Arab-Israeli Conflict

By Roberto Miguel Rodriguez

Book Outline

Introduction:

In this comprehensive history of the Arab-Israeli conflict, we delve into the intricate web of events, ideologies, and power dynamics that have shaped the region for over a century. Addressed to historians and scholars specializing in this field, "From Balfour to Oslo" aims to provide a nuanced understanding of the conflict by exploring various key themes and influences.

The History of the Arab-Israeli Conflict

This chapter lays the foundation for our exploration, tracing the origins of the conflict from the Balfour Declaration in 1917 to the signing of the Oslo Accords in 1993. We examine the historical context, including the aftermath of World War I, the League of Nations mandate system, and the rise of Zionism and Arab nationalism.

The Impact of British Colonialism on the Arab-Israeli Conflict

Here, we delve into the role of British colonialism in shaping the conflict. We analyze the consequences of British policies, such as the Sykes-Picot Agreement, the White Paper of 1939, and the partition plan of 1947. Additionally, we explore the repercussions of British military presence and their impact on local dynamics.

The Role of Religious and Cultural Differences in the Arab-Israeli Conflict

This chapter investigates the role of religious and cultural disparities in fueling the conflict. We examine the historical significance of Jerusalem, the competing claims to the land by Jews and Arabs, and the impact of religious extremism on the peace process.

The Influence of External Powers on the Arab-Israeli Conflict

In this section, we analyze the impact of external powers, particularly the United States and the Soviet Union, on the Arab-Israeli conflict. We explore how Cold War rivalries shaped alliances, arms agreements, and diplomatic efforts, and their influence on the peace process.

The Role of Palestinian Nationalism in the Arab-Israeli Conflict

Here, we delve into the development of Palestinian nationalism as a key factor in the conflict. We examine the rise of the Palestinian Liberation Organization (PLO), their struggle for statehood, and the impact of their political and military strategies.

The Impact of the Israeli Settlement Movement on the Arab-Israeli Conflict

This chapter explores the contentious issue of Israeli settlements in the occupied territories and their impact on the conflict. We analyze the historical expansion of settlements, their legality under international law, and their implications for future negotiations.

Territorial Disputes and Border Conflicts in the Arab-Israeli Conflict

In this section, we examine the territorial disputes and border conflicts that have plagued the region. We explore key flashpoints such as the Golan Heights, West Bank, Gaza Strip, and the Sinai Peninsula, analyzing their historical significance and their impact on the peace process.

The Impact of the Six-Day War on the Arab-Israeli Conflict

This chapter delves into the consequences of the Six-Day War in 1967, a pivotal event that reshaped the dynamics of the conflict. We explore the territorial gains made by Israel, the displacement of Palestinian populations, and the long-term implications for peace negotiations.

The Role of International Organizations in Resolving the Arab-Israeli Conflict

Here, we analyze the role of international organizations, particularly the United Nations and the Arab League, in attempting to resolve the conflict. We examine the successes and failures of their diplomatic efforts, including the various peace plans proposed over the years.

The Impact of the Camp David Accords on the Arab-Israeli Conflict

This chapter explores the impact of the Camp David Accords in 1978, a significant breakthrough in the peace process. We analyze the negotiations between Egypt, Israel, and the United States, the implications for regional stability, and the challenges that remained unresolved.

The Influence of Terrorism and Guerrilla Warfare in the Arab-Israeli Conflict

In the final chapter, we explore the influence of terrorism and guerrilla warfare on the conflict. We analyze the strategies employed by groups such as Hamas and Hezbollah, the impact of suicide bombings, and the challenges they pose to the peace process.

Conclusion:

"From Balfour to Oslo: A Comprehensive History of the Arab-Israeli Conflict" offers a multifaceted analysis of this complex and enduring conflict. By examining key historical events, the role of external powers, religious and cultural differences, and the impact of various factors on the peace process, this book provides historians with a comprehensive understanding of the conflict and its ongoing implications.

Chapter 1: The History of the Arab-Israeli Conflict

The Origins of the Arab-Israeli Conflict

The Arab-Israeli conflict is a complex and deeply rooted conflict that has its origins in a number of historical factors. Understanding the origins of this conflict is crucial for historians studying the history of the Arab-Israeli conflict and its various facets.

One significant factor in the origins of the Arab-Israeli conflict is the impact of British colonialism. After the First World War, the League of Nations entrusted Britain with the mandate to administer Palestine, leading to the establishment of a Jewish homeland. This decision, known as the Balfour Declaration, laid the groundwork for the conflict by favoring Jewish settlers over the indigenous Arab population.

Religious and cultural differences have also played a crucial role in fueling the Arab-Israeli conflict. The conflict is deeply rooted in the clash between Jewish and Arab nationalism, as well as religious disputes over control of holy sites in Jerusalem. The Zionist movement sought to establish a Jewish state in Palestine, which was met with resistance from Arab nationalists who feared losing their own claims to the land.

External powers, particularly the United States and the Soviet Union, have had a significant influence on the Arab-Israeli conflict. Both superpowers supported different sides, with the United States largely backing Israel and the Soviet Union supporting Arab states. This external involvement has further complicated the conflict and made it difficult to reach a lasting resolution.

The role of Palestinian nationalism has also been instrumental in the Arab-Israeli conflict. The rise of Palestinian nationalism in the 20th century, coupled with the displacement of Palestinians during the creation of Israel, has fueled ongoing tensions and resistance against Israeli occupation.

The impact of the Israeli settlement movement cannot be overlooked in the Arab-Israeli conflict. Israeli settlements in the occupied territories have been a major source of contention, as they have led to territorial disputes and border conflicts, further straining relations between Israelis and Palestinians.

The Six-Day War in 1967 had a profound impact on the Arab-Israeli conflict. Israel's victory in this war led to the occupation of the West Bank, Gaza Strip, Sinai Peninsula, and the Golan Heights, leading to further territorial disputes and resistance from Arab nations.

International organizations, such as the United Nations and the Arab League, have played a role in attempting to resolve the Arab-Israeli conflict. However, their efforts have often been hindered by the complexities and deep-seated divisions between the parties involved.

The Camp David Accords in 1978 marked a significant milestone in the Arab-Israeli conflict. This peace agreement between Israel and Egypt demonstrated the potential for resolving the conflict through diplomacy, although it did not address the broader issues of Palestinian statehood.

Terrorism and guerrilla warfare have also had a profound impact on the Arab-Israeli conflict. Groups such as the Palestine Liberation Organization (PLO) and Hamas have used violence as a means of resistance against Israeli occupation, further perpetuating the cycle of violence and mistrust.

In conclusion, the origins of the Arab-Israeli conflict can be traced back to a multitude of factors, including British colonialism, religious and cultural differences, external powers, Palestinian nationalism, territorial disputes, and the impact of significant events such as the Six-Day War. Understanding these origins is crucial for historians seeking to grasp the complexities of the Arab-Israeli conflict and the various dynamics that have shaped its history.

The Early Zionist Movement

The early Zionist movement played a pivotal role in shaping the Arab-Israeli conflict, and its roots can be traced back to the late 19th century. This subchapter explores the origins and development of Zionism, highlighting its impact on the Arab-Israeli conflict.

Zionism emerged as a response to increasing anti-Semitism in Europe, with Jewish intellectuals and activists seeking a homeland for the Jewish people. Influenced by nationalist movements of the time, Zionists believed that only through the establishment of a Jewish state could Jews escape persecution and achieve self-determination. The movement gained traction under the leadership of Theodor Herzl, who advocated for a Jewish state in Palestine.

However, the Zionist vision faced significant challenges. The land of Palestine was not empty, but rather inhabited by a predominantly Arab population. As Jewish immigration to Palestine increased, tensions between Jewish settlers and Arab natives grew. The clash between nationalist aspirations and the reality on the ground laid the foundation for the Arab-Israeli conflict.

The British colonial presence in Palestine further complicated the situation. With the issuance of the Balfour Declaration in 1917, Britain expressed support for the establishment of a Jewish homeland in Palestine. This declaration, while celebrated by Zionists, was met with fierce opposition from the Arab population. The impact of British colonialism on the Arab-Israeli conflict cannot be overstated, as it fueled Arab resentment towards both the British and the Zionist project.

Religious and cultural differences also played a significant role in the conflict. Both Jews and Arabs had deep historical and religious ties to the land, making claims to the territory deeply rooted in their respective identities. This clash of narratives and the attachment to sacred sites further exacerbated tensions between the two communities.

External powers, particularly the United States and the Soviet Union, exerted influence on the Arab-Israeli conflict. The U.S. emerged as a key supporter of Israel, providing military aid and diplomatic backing. The Soviet Union, on the other hand, supported Arab states, viewing them as potential allies in the Cold War. These external alliances added another layer of complexity to the conflict.

The early Zionist movement also had a profound impact on Palestinian nationalism. The growing sense of displacement and dispossession among Palestinians led to the emergence of a national consciousness, with leaders such as Haj Amin al-Husseini advocating for Palestinian self-determination.

The Israeli settlement movement further fueled tensions in the conflict. Jewish settlements in the occupied territories, seen as illegal by the international community, became a major obstacle to peace negotiations and a source of continuous friction between Israelis and Palestinians.

The territorial disputes and border conflicts in the Arab-Israeli conflict have been a recurring theme. The 1948 Arab-Israeli War, the Six-Day War in 1967, and subsequent conflicts have resulted in territorial gains and losses for both sides, further deepening the divide.

International organizations, such as the United Nations and the Arab League, have played a role in attempting to resolve the conflict. However, their efforts have been met with limited success, as both sides remain entrenched in their positions.

The impact of the Camp David Accords in 1978 and subsequent peace agreements between Israel and its Arab neighbors have had a mixed impact on the Arab-Israeli conflict. While they provided a framework for peaceful coexistence, the core issues of the conflict, such as the status of Jerusalem and the right of return for Palestinian refugees, remain unresolved.

Terrorism and guerrilla warfare have also shaped the Arab-Israeli conflict. Palestinian militant groups, such as Hamas and Hezbollah, have employed these tactics in their struggle against Israel, further complicating efforts to achieve a lasting peace.

In conclusion, the early Zionist movement played a pivotal role in shaping the Arab-Israeli conflict. The impact of British colonialism, religious and cultural differences, external powers, Palestinian nationalism, Israeli settlements, territorial disputes, and international organizations have all contributed to the complexities of the conflict. The influence of the Six-Day War, the Camp David Accords, and the role of terrorism and guerrilla warfare have further shaped the ongoing struggle for peace in the region. Understanding the historical context and dynamics of these factors is crucial for historians studying the Arab-Israeli conflict.

British Mandate in Palestine

The British Mandate in Palestine was a significant chapter in the history of the Arab-Israeli conflict. Following the defeat of the Ottoman Empire in World War I, the League of Nations granted Britain the Mandate over Palestine in 1920. This decision was influenced by the Balfour Declaration, a British policy statement that supported the establishment of a Jewish homeland in Palestine.

During the Mandate period, Britain faced numerous challenges in trying to balance the interests of both Jewish and Arab communities. The impact of British colonialism on the Arab-Israeli conflict cannot be underestimated. The British administration implemented policies that favored Jewish immigration and land acquisition, leading to increased tensions with the Arab population. These policies were perceived as a betrayal by the Palestinians, who had hoped for independence and self-determination.

Religious and cultural differences played a significant role in exacerbating the conflict during the Mandate period. The clash between Jewish and Arab nationalisms, fueled by religious and cultural differences, intensified the struggle for control over Palestine. Both sides claimed historical and religious ties to the land, which further complicated any attempts at compromise.

External powers, such as the United States and the Soviet Union, also had an influence on the Arab-Israeli conflict during the Mandate period. The United States emerged as a key supporter of the Zionist movement, while the Soviet Union supported Arab nationalist aspirations. These external powers provided political, financial, and military support to their respective allies, further fueling the conflict.

Palestinian nationalism emerged as a significant factor during the Mandate period. The Palestinians, who felt marginalized and betrayed by the British, began to assert their own national identity and demand self-determination. This led to the rise of various nationalist movements and organizations, which played a crucial role in shaping the Arab-Israeli conflict.

The Israeli settlement movement, which started during the Mandate period, has had a lasting impact on the conflict. Jewish settlers established communities in Palestine, often leading to disputes over land and resources with the local Arab population. The settlement movement continues to be a contentious issue and a major obstacle to peace negotiations.

Territorial disputes and border conflicts were prevalent throughout the Mandate period. Both Jewish and Arab militias engaged in violence and fought for control over territory. These conflicts laid the groundwork for the larger territorial disputes that would follow, particularly after the establishment of the State of Israel in 1948.

The Six-Day War in 1967 had a profound impact on the Arab-Israeli conflict. Israel's swift victory and subsequent occupation of the West Bank, Gaza Strip, Sinai Peninsula, and Golan Heights created new dynamics and further complicated efforts to resolve the conflict.

International organizations, such as the United Nations and the Arab League, have played a role in attempting to resolve the Arab-Israeli conflict. The United Nations passed resolutions and established peacekeeping missions, but these efforts have often been hampered by political divisions and competing interests.

The Camp David Accords in 1978 marked a significant development in the Arab-Israeli conflict. The agreement between Israel and Egypt paved the way for peace negotiations and the recognition of Israel's right to exist by Arab states. However, it did not address the broader Palestinian question, leading to continued conflict.

Terrorism and guerrilla warfare have also shaped the Arab-Israeli conflict. Palestinian militant groups, such as the Palestine Liberation Organization (PLO), resorted to violence to achieve their political goals. Acts of terrorism and guerrilla warfare have had a significant impact on the conflict, further escalating tensions and hindering peace efforts.

Overall, the British Mandate in Palestine played a crucial role in shaping the Arab-Israeli conflict. The impact of British colonialism, the role of religious and cultural differences, the influence of external powers, the rise of Palestinian nationalism, the Israeli settlement movement, territorial disputes, the Six-Day War, international organizations, the Camp David Accords, and terrorism and guerrilla warfare all contributed to the complexity and longevity of the conflict. Understanding these dynamics is crucial for historians studying the history of the Arab-Israeli conflict.

The Balfour Declaration and its Consequences

The Balfour Declaration, issued by the British government in 1917, holds significant importance in the history of the Arab-Israeli conflict. Addressed to Lord Rothschild, a prominent British Zionist leader, the declaration expressed the British government's support for the establishment of a "national home for the Jewish people" in Palestine. This chapter explores the consequences of this declaration and its far-reaching impact on the Arab-Israeli conflict.

The Balfour Declaration marked a turning point in the conflict as it provided the Zionist movement with an official recognition and endorsement from a major world power. However, this support for Jewish national aspirations came at the expense of the indigenous Arab population of Palestine. The declaration disregarded the rights and aspirations of the Arab majority, leading to a deep sense of betrayal and resentment among the Arab communities.

The declaration's consequences were far-reaching. It set in motion a series of events that fundamentally altered the demographic, political, and territorial dynamics of the region. The influx of Jewish settlers, encouraged by the British government, led to clashes between Jewish and Arab communities, further fueling tensions and sowing the seeds of future conflicts.

The Balfour Declaration also had a profound impact on the role of external powers in the Arab-Israeli conflict. The United States and the Soviet Union, seeking to advance their own interests in the region, became increasingly involved, providing military, financial, and political support to the respective sides. This external interference exacerbated the conflict, prolonging its duration and complexity.

The declaration also significantly influenced the rise of Palestinian nationalism. The Palestinian Arabs, feeling marginalized and oppressed, began to assert their own national identity and demand self-determination. This led to the emergence of various Palestinian nationalist movements, which would play a crucial role in shaping the conflict in the decades to come.

Furthermore, the Balfour Declaration laid the foundation for the Israeli settlement movement, resulting in the establishment of numerous Jewish settlements in the occupied territories. These settlements have been a major source of contention, further complicating efforts to reach a peaceful resolution to the conflict.

In conclusion, the Balfour Declaration and its consequences have played a pivotal role in shaping the Arab-Israeli conflict. Its endorsement of Jewish national aspirations, coupled with the disregard for Arab rights, has fueled animosity and conflict in the region. The declaration's impact on external powers, Palestinian nationalism, the settlement movement, and territorial disputes underscores its enduring significance in the complex history of the conflict.

Chapter 2: The Impact of British Colonialism on the Arab-Israeli Conflict

British Policies in Palestine

The British policies in Palestine during the early 20th century played a crucial role in shaping the Arab-Israeli conflict. As historians, it is essential to understand the impact of British colonialism on this conflict, the role of religious and cultural differences, the influence of external powers, and the significance of Palestinian nationalism.

Under the Balfour Declaration of 1917, the British government expressed support for the establishment of a "national home for the Jewish people" in Palestine. This declaration had far-reaching consequences, as it led to an influx of Jewish immigrants and the establishment of Jewish settlements in the region. However, this policy also ignited tensions between the Jewish and Arab populations, laying the foundation for the conflict.

The British Mandate in Palestine, which lasted from 1920 to 1948, further exacerbated the conflict. The Mandate's contradictory promises to both Jews and Arabs created a volatile situation, as both groups had competing national aspirations. The British struggled to maintain control and balance the interests of these two communities, ultimately failing to find a satisfactory solution.

The influence of external powers, such as the United States and the Soviet Union, also shaped the Arab-Israeli conflict. The United States emerged as a key player in the conflict after World War II, supporting the establishment of the State of Israel. The Soviet Union, on the other hand, backed Arab states, fueling tensions and escalating the conflict.

Religious and cultural differences between Jews and Arabs have long been a point of contention in the Arab-Israeli conflict. The clash between Judaism and Islam, exacerbated by the presence of holy sites in Jerusalem, has fueled hostility and contributed to the intractability of the conflict.

The emergence of Palestinian nationalism in the mid-20th century further complicated the conflict. Palestinians sought self-determination and independence, leading to numerous uprisings and resistance movements. The British policies, including restrictions on Arab political aspirations, contributed to the growth of Palestinian nationalism and its role in the conflict.

The impact of the Israeli settlement movement on the Arab-Israeli conflict cannot be understated. Israeli settlements in the occupied territories have been a major source of tension, as they are seen as an obstacle to a peaceful resolution. The settlement movement has led to territorial disputes and border conflicts, further perpetuating the cycle of violence.

The Six-Day War in 1967 had a profound impact on the Arab-Israeli conflict. Israel's swift military victory and subsequent occupation of the West Bank, Gaza Strip, and East Jerusalem transformed the conflict and shaped subsequent negotiations and peace processes.

International organizations, such as the United Nations and the Arab League, have played a role in attempting to resolve the Arab-Israeli conflict. The United Nations has passed numerous resolutions calling for a peaceful settlement, while the Arab League has supported the Palestinian cause and advocated for their rights.

The Camp David Accords in 1978 marked a significant turning point in the conflict. The peace agreement between Israel and Egypt, brokered by the United States, showed the potential for diplomatic solutions and led to the normalization of relations between the two countries.

Lastly, terrorism and guerrilla warfare have had a profound impact on the Arab-Israeli conflict. Groups such as Hamas and Hezbollah have conducted attacks against Israel, while Israel has responded with military force. These acts of violence have further deepened the animosity between the parties involved, making a peaceful resolution even more challenging.

In conclusion, the British policies in Palestine, alongside the interplay of religious and cultural differences, external powers, Palestinian nationalism, Israeli settlements, territorial disputes, and the impact of events such as the Six-Day War and Camp David Accords, have all shaped the Arab-Israeli conflict. Understanding these factors is crucial for historians seeking to comprehend the complexities and dynamics of this enduring conflict.

Arab Nationalism and Resistance

Arab nationalism played a significant role in the Arab-Israeli conflict, shaping the resistance movements and influencing the course of events. This subchapter explores the historical context, causes, and consequences of Arab nationalism, as well as its impact on the conflict.

Arab nationalism emerged in the late 19th and early 20th centuries as a response to the increasing Western influence and the dismantling of the Ottoman Empire. It sought to unite Arab peoples under a common identity and secure independence from foreign powers, including the British and French colonial rulers. The rise of Arab nationalism in the region had a profound impact on the Arab-Israeli conflict, fueling resistance movements against the establishment of a Jewish homeland in Palestine.

The Arab-Israeli conflict was significantly influenced by the impact of British colonialism. With the issuance of the Balfour Declaration in 1917, which supported the establishment of a Jewish national home in Palestine, tensions between Arabs and Jews escalated. The British Mandate period witnessed a rise in Arab nationalism and resistance against Jewish immigration, leading to violent clashes and uprisings.

Religious and cultural differences also played a crucial role in fueling the Arab-Israeli conflict. The conflict is deeply rooted in the historical, religious, and cultural connections of both Arabs and Jews to the land of Palestine. These differences contributed to the polarization between the two communities, making any resolution or compromise a daunting task.

The influence of external powers, such as the United States and the Soviet Union, further complicated the conflict. The Cold War rivalry between these superpowers saw them backing different sides, with the United States supporting Israel and the Soviet Union supporting Arab states. This external involvement exacerbated tensions and hindered peaceful resolutions.

Palestinian nationalism emerged as a significant force in the Arab-Israeli conflict. The Palestinian Liberation Organization (PLO), led by Yasser Arafat, became the voice of Palestinian aspirations for statehood and self-determination. The PLO's armed resistance and political strategies shaped the conflict and brought international attention to the Palestinian cause.

Territorial disputes and border conflicts have been major flashpoints in the Arab-Israeli conflict. From the 1948 Arab-Israeli War to the Six-Day War in 1967 and subsequent conflicts, disputes over land and borders have been significant drivers of tension and violence in the region.

The role of international organizations, such as the United Nations and the Arab League, in resolving the conflict has been both crucial and challenging. While these organizations have made efforts to promote peace, their resolutions have often been disregarded or rejected by the parties involved.

The impact of the Camp David Accords between Egypt and Israel in 1978 had a profound effect on the conflict. While it led to the normalization of relations between Egypt and Israel, it failed to address the core issues of the conflict, such as the status of Jerusalem and the rights of Palestinian refugees.

Terrorism and guerrilla warfare have also played a significant role in the Arab-Israeli conflict. Groups like Hamas and Hezbollah have resorted to violent means to further their political objectives, further complicating efforts to achieve a lasting peace.

In conclusion, Arab nationalism and resistance have shaped the Arab-Israeli conflict in profound ways. The historical context, the impact of British colonialism, religious and cultural differences, external powers' involvement, the role of Palestinian nationalism, territorial disputes, and border conflicts, the Six-Day War, international organizations' efforts, the Camp David Accords, and the influence of terrorism and guerrilla warfare have all contributed to the complexities of the conflict. Understanding these dynamics is crucial for historians studying the Arab-Israeli conflict and its evolution over time.

Jewish Immigration and Settlements

The subchapter on Jewish Immigration and Settlements delves into the significant role played by Jewish immigration and settlement in the Arab-Israeli conflict. This chapter explores how the influx of Jewish immigrants and their establishment of settlements in Palestine during the late 19th and early 20th centuries laid the foundation for the conflict that continues to this day.

The chapter begins by examining the historical context that led to Jewish immigration to Palestine. It highlights the rise of Zionism, a political movement advocating for the establishment of a Jewish homeland, and the impact of increasing anti-Semitism in Europe, particularly during the late 19th century. These factors prompted many Jewish individuals and families to seek refuge in Palestine, which was under Ottoman rule at the time.

The chapter then explores the establishment of Jewish settlements, known as "kibbutzim" and "moshavim," and their impact on the Arab population. It discusses the tensions that arose as Jewish settlers purchased land from Arab landowners, leading to clashes over land ownership and economic disparities. The chapter also examines the influence of British colonial policies, such as the Balfour Declaration of 1917, which expressed support for a Jewish homeland in Palestine, and the subsequent British Mandate, which facilitated Jewish immigration and settlement.

Furthermore, the chapter analyzes the consequences of Jewish immigration and settlement on the Arab-Israeli conflict. It explores how these developments contributed to the rise of Palestinian nationalism, as Arab Palestinians began to perceive Jewish immigration as a threat to their national identity and rights. This section also discusses the territorial disputes and border conflicts resulting from the establishment of Jewish settlements, which have been central issues in the Arab-Israeli conflict.

Additionally, the chapter touches upon the role of external powers, such as the United States and the Soviet Union, in influencing the Arab-Israeli conflict. It examines how these nations supported either the Jewish or Arab side, often based on their own strategic interests.

This subchapter concludes by highlighting the ongoing impact of Jewish immigration and settlement on the Arab-Israeli conflict. It discusses the continued expansion of Israeli settlements in the West Bank, which has been a major obstacle to peace negotiations and a source of contention between Israelis and Palestinians.

Overall, this section sheds light on the complex historical dynamics surrounding Jewish immigration and settlement, and their profound influence on the Arab-Israeli conflict. It provides historians with a comprehensive understanding of the origins and consequences of these developments, as well as their ongoing implications for resolving the conflict.

Arab Reactions to British Rule

The era of British rule in the Arab world left a lasting impact on the Arab-Israeli conflict. This subchapter will delve into the various reactions of the Arab population to British colonialism, shedding light on the historical context that shaped the conflict.

The Arab response to British rule was characterized by a complex mix of resistance, collaboration, and ambivalence. Many Arabs, particularly those in Palestine, felt betrayed by the British government's contradictory promises regarding the establishment of a Jewish homeland. This betrayal sparked widespread protests and uprisings, such as the Arab Revolt of 1936-1939, which was met with brutal force by the British authorities.

Religious and cultural differences also played a significant role in the Arab response to British rule. The Arab population, predominantly Muslim, saw the British presence as a threat to their religious and cultural identity. The British administration's support for Jewish immigration and settlement further exacerbated these tensions, leading to increased hostility towards both the British and the Jewish population.

External powers, namely the United States and the Soviet Union, exerted their influence on the Arab-Israeli conflict during the British rule. The United States, in particular, played a crucial role in shaping the conflict through its support for the Zionist movement. This support further fueled Arab resentment towards the British and their perceived bias.

Throughout this period, Palestinian nationalism emerged as a powerful force, driven by the desire for self-determination and resistance against British rule. The Arab population sought to establish an independent Palestinian state, and their struggle for sovereignty became intertwined with the larger Arab-Israeli conflict.

Territorial disputes and border conflicts were inevitable consequences of British rule. The British administration's arbitrary drawing of borders and conflicting promises to different parties created a volatile environment, laying the groundwork for future conflicts.

The impact of the Six-Day War cannot be understated in the Arab-Israeli conflict. The swift Israeli victory and subsequent occupation of Arab territories profoundly affected Arab perceptions and strategies. It fueled a rise in terrorism and guerrilla warfare as means of resistance against Israeli occupation.

International organizations, such as the United Nations and the Arab League, played a significant role in attempting to resolve the Arab-Israeli conflict during the British rule. However, their efforts often fell short, and the conflict continued to escalate.

The Camp David Accords marked a turning point in the conflict, but their impact was mixed. While they established a framework for peace between Israel and Egypt, they failed to address the broader Arab-Israeli conflict, leaving Palestinian aspirations unfulfilled.

In conclusion, the Arab reaction to British rule was a complex mix of resistance, collaboration, and ambivalence. The impact of religious and cultural differences, external powers, Palestinian nationalism, territorial disputes, and border conflicts shaped the conflict during this period. The Six-Day War, the role of international organizations, and the influence of terrorism and guerrilla warfare further deepened the complexity of the Arab-Israeli conflict during British rule. Understanding these reactions is crucial in comprehending the historical roots and ongoing dynamics of the Arab-Israeli conflict.

Chapter 3: The Role of Religious and Cultural Differences in the Arab-Israeli Conflict

Religious and Cultural Tensions in the Region

The Arab-Israeli conflict is a complex and multifaceted issue that has deep historical roots. One of the key factors contributing to this conflict is the religious and cultural tensions in the region. These tensions have played a significant role in shaping the conflict and have often exacerbated existing divisions.

Religion, particularly the clash between Judaism and Islam, has been a central element in the Arab-Israeli conflict. Both Israelis and Palestinians have strong religious affiliations, with Jerusalem being a holy site for both Jews and Muslims. The struggle for control over religious sites, such as the Western Wall and Al-Aqsa Mosque, has fueled tensions and acts of violence. Additionally, religious beliefs have influenced political ideologies and nationalist movements, further entrenching the conflict.

Cultural differences have also contributed to the ongoing tensions in the region. The Arab and Jewish communities have distinct cultural traditions, languages, and social norms. These differences have often led to misunderstandings and mistrust between the two groups. The Arab-Israeli conflict has deep historical roots, and cultural differences have been passed down through generations, perpetuating the divide.

External powers, such as the United States and the Soviet Union, have also played a significant role in exacerbating religious and cultural tensions in the region. These powers have often aligned themselves with one side of the conflict, providing military and economic support. This external intervention has further fueled animosity between Israelis and

Palestinians, as each side perceives the other as being backed by a powerful external force.

The impact of the Israeli settlement movement on the Arab-Israeli conflict cannot be understated. The establishment of Israeli settlements in the occupied territories has led to increased tensions and territorial disputes. Palestinians view these settlements as illegal and a barrier to a future independent state, while Israelis argue for their legitimacy based on historical and religious claims.

Territorial disputes and border conflicts have been a constant source of tension in the Arab-Israeli conflict. The 1967 Six-Day War, in particular, had a profound impact on the conflict by changing the territorial landscape and exacerbating existing grievances. The war resulted in Israel gaining control over the West Bank, Gaza Strip, and East Jerusalem, which further complicated the prospects for a peaceful resolution.

The role of international organizations, such as the United Nations and the Arab League, in resolving the Arab-Israeli conflict has been both constructive and contentious. While these organizations have been involved in peace negotiations and proposed resolutions, their efforts have often been hindered by political divisions and competing interests.

The influence of the Camp David Accords and subsequent peace agreements on the Arab-Israeli conflict cannot be overlooked. These agreements, particularly the Camp David Accords between Israel and Egypt, have had a significant impact on regional dynamics and the prospects for peace. However, they have also faced criticism from some factions, who argue that they did not adequately address the core issues of the conflict.

Finally, terrorism and guerrilla warfare have had a profound impact on the Arab-Israeli conflict. Acts of violence committed by both Palestinians and Israelis have further deepened the divide between the two communities and hindered efforts for reconciliation. Moreover, these acts of terrorism have often been used by external powers to further their own interests, perpetuating the cycle of violence.

In conclusion, religious and cultural tensions have played a central role in the Arab-Israeli conflict. These tensions, combined with the influence of external powers, territorial disputes, and acts of violence, have contributed to the ongoing conflict. Resolving this conflict will require addressing these deep-rooted divisions and finding a way to bridge the religious and cultural gaps between Israelis and Palestinians.

Zionism and Jewish Identity

Zionism, the political movement advocating for the establishment of a Jewish homeland in Palestine, has played a significant role in shaping Jewish identity and the Arab-Israeli conflict. Understanding the relationship between Zionism and Jewish identity is crucial for comprehending the complex historical dynamics that have contributed to the ongoing conflict.

At its core, Zionism emerged as a response to the rise of anti-Semitism in Europe during the late 19th and early 20th centuries. The movement aimed to provide a solution to the persecution and discrimination faced by Jews by establishing a Jewish state. For many Jews, Zionism became a central component of their identity, offering a sense of belonging and security in a world that often rejected them.

However, the Zionist project also faced opposition from various corners, including the Arab population of Palestine. The establishment of a Jewish homeland inevitably clashed with the aspirations of the Arab majority, who saw their rights and claims to the land threatened.

The interplay between Jewish identity and Arab nationalism has been a central theme throughout the Arab-Israeli conflict.

British colonialism, which controlled Palestine from 1917 to 1948, further complicated the situation. The Balfour Declaration of 1917, which expressed British support for the establishment of a Jewish homeland, had a profound impact on the conflict. While it provided a significant boost to the Zionist cause, it also fueled Arab resentment and mistrust towards British policies.

Religious and cultural differences have also significantly influenced the Arab-Israeli conflict. Jerusalem, a city of immense religious significance to both Jews and Muslims, has been a focal point of contention. The clash between Jewish and Palestinian nationalisms has been intertwined with the desire to control and preserve religious sites, exacerbating tensions between the two communities.

External powers, such as the United States and the Soviet Union, have played a significant role in shaping the conflict. The United States emerged as a staunch ally of Israel, providing crucial military, economic, and political support. Meanwhile, the Soviet Union backed Arab states, contributing to the polarization and militarization of the conflict.

The impact of the Israeli settlement movement on the Arab-Israeli conflict cannot be overlooked. Israeli settlements in the occupied territories have been a major point of contention, hindering peace negotiations and deepening Palestinian grievances.

Territorial disputes and border conflicts have been a recurring feature of the Arab-Israeli conflict. The Six-Day War of 1967, in which Israel captured significant territories, including the West Bank and Gaza Strip, dramatically altered the geopolitical landscape, further fueling the conflict.

International organizations, such as the United Nations and the Arab League, have attempted to mediate and resolve the conflict, but with limited success. The Camp David Accords of 1978, which led to a peace treaty between Israel and Egypt, marked a notable breakthrough but failed to address the broader issues at the heart of the conflict.

Terrorism and guerrilla warfare have also played a significant role in the Arab-Israeli conflict. From the Palestinian Liberation Organization to Hamas, armed groups have employed violence as a means to resist Israeli occupation, leading to cycles of retaliation and bloodshed.

In conclusion, the relationship between Zionism and Jewish identity has profoundly influenced the Arab-Israeli conflict. Understanding this connection, along with the impact of British colonialism, religious and cultural differences, external powers, Palestinian nationalism, Israeli settlements, territorial disputes, the Six-Day War, international organizations, and terrorism, is crucial for historians seeking a comprehensive understanding of this protracted and complex conflict.

Arab Nationalism and Islamic Identity

Arab Nationalism and Islamic Identity have played significant roles in shaping the Arab-Israeli conflict throughout history. This subchapter examines the impact of these ideologies on the conflict, shedding light on their historical development and their influence on various aspects of the conflict.

Arab Nationalism emerged in the late 19th and early 20th centuries as a response to Western imperialism and the division of Arab lands by colonial powers, notably the British. It sought to unite Arabs across different regions, emphasizing a shared Arab identity and the desire for self-rule. This movement was fueled by a sense of frustration and discontentment among Arabs, who sought to regain their independence and control over their own affairs.

In the context of the Arab-Israeli conflict, Arab Nationalism became a unifying force against the establishment of a Jewish state in Palestine. Arab nationalist leaders, such as Gamal Abdel Nasser of Egypt, championed the Palestinian cause and rallied Arab nations against Israel. They argued that the establishment of Israel was a violation of Arab sovereignty and an infringement on the rights of the Palestinian people.

Islamic Identity, on the other hand, draws on the principles and values of Islam to shape political and social identities. It emphasizes the importance of the Muslim ummah (community) and the protection of Islamic holy sites, including Jerusalem. Islamic identity has been instrumentalized in the Arab-Israeli conflict, with religious leaders and organizations playing a significant role in mobilizing support for the Palestinian cause and opposing Israeli policies.

Furthermore, external powers have exerted their influence on the Arab-Israeli conflict, often exacerbating tensions between Arab nations and Israel. The United States, for instance, has historically supported Israel, providing military aid and diplomatic backing. Similarly, the Soviet Union aligned itself with Arab states, hoping to gain influence in the region. The involvement of these external powers has shaped the dynamics of the conflict and influenced its trajectory.

This subchapter also explores the role of Palestinian nationalism in the Arab-Israeli conflict, examining the struggle for self-determination and statehood. It delves into the impact of the Israeli settlement movement on the conflict, discussing how the expansion of Israeli settlements in the occupied territories has hindered the prospects for peace and fueled tensions.

Territorial disputes and border conflicts have been recurring themes in the Arab-Israeli conflict, and this subchapter examines their historical context and implications. It also delves into the impact of the Six-Day

War, a pivotal event that reshaped the geopolitical landscape of the region and intensified the conflict.

The subchapter also explores the role of international organizations, such as the United Nations and the Arab League, in resolving the Arab-Israeli conflict. It discusses their involvement, initiatives, and the challenges they have faced in their pursuit of peace.

Finally, this subchapter sheds light on the influence of terrorism and guerrilla warfare in the Arab-Israeli conflict, examining how these tactics have been employed by various groups to achieve their goals and the impact they have had on the overall conflict.

Overall, this subchapter provides a comprehensive overview of Arab Nationalism and Islamic Identity in the context of the Arab-Israeli conflict, highlighting their historical development and their impact on various aspects of the conflict. It offers historians invaluable insights into the complex dynamics and multifaceted nature of this enduring conflict.

Clash of Narratives: Historical and Sacred Sites

Throughout the history of the Arab-Israeli conflict, one of the key elements that has fueled tensions and divisions between the two sides is the clash over historical and sacred sites. These sites hold immense religious, cultural, and historical significance for both Palestinians and Israelis, representing the deep-rooted attachment to the land and the narratives that have shaped their identities.

One of the most contentious sites is Jerusalem, a city revered by Jews, Christians, and Muslims alike. The historical and religious significance of Jerusalem has made it a focal point of the conflict, with both sides vying for control and sovereignty over the city. The Western Wall, the Church of the Holy Sepulchre, and the Al-Aqsa Mosque are just a few of the holy sites that have been at the center of clashes and disputes.

Another flashpoint is the city of Hebron, where the Tomb of the Patriarchs is located. This site is revered by both Jews and Muslims as the burial place of Abraham, Isaac, and Jacob. However, the presence of Israeli settlements in Hebron has created tensions and conflicts, as Palestinians view these settlements as a violation of their rights and a hindrance to their aspirations for statehood.

The impact of external powers, particularly the United States and the Soviet Union, on the Arab-Israeli conflict cannot be understated. These powers have often played a decisive role in shaping the narratives surrounding historical and sacred sites. For example, the United States' recognition of Jerusalem as Israel's capital in 2017 sparked widespread condemnation from Palestinians and Arab nations, as it undermined the Palestinian claim to East Jerusalem as their future capital.

Furthermore, the role of international organizations, such as the United Nations and the Arab League, in resolving the conflict has been instrumental. These organizations have attempted to address the clash over historical and sacred sites through various resolutions and peace initiatives. However, their efforts have often been stymied by the deeply entrenched narratives and the competing claims of both sides.

In conclusion, the clash over historical and sacred sites is a crucial aspect of the Arab-Israeli conflict. The deep religious, cultural, and historical significance of these sites has fueled tensions and divisions between Palestinians and Israelis. The influence of external powers, the role of international organizations, and the impact of the Israeli settlement movement have all contributed to shaping the narratives surrounding these sites. Understanding the complexities and sensitivities associated with historical and sacred sites is essential for historians studying the Arab-Israeli conflict and its ramifications on the region.

Chapter 4: The Influence of External Powers on the Arab-Israeli Conflict

United States and its Support for Israel

The United States has played a significant role in the Arab-Israeli conflict, particularly in its support for Israel. From the early stages of the conflict to the present day, the United States has been a key ally of Israel, providing political, military, and economic support. This subchapter aims to delve into the historical context and examine the reasons behind the United States' unwavering support for Israel.

One of the primary factors shaping the United States' support for Israel is the impact of British colonialism on the Arab-Israeli conflict. The British Mandate in Palestine, which lasted from 1920 to 1948, laid the groundwork for the establishment of a Jewish homeland. This contributed to the rise of Zionism and the eventual creation of the state of Israel. The United States, influenced by its historical ties with Britain, aligned its policies with the Zionist cause.

Religious and cultural differences have also played a significant role in the conflict. The United States, as a predominantly Christian nation, has had strong ties to Israel, which has deep religious significance for Jews worldwide. This religious connection has fostered a sense of solidarity and empathy between the two nations.

Furthermore, the influence of external powers, such as the United States and the Soviet Union, has had a profound impact on the Arab-Israeli conflict. During the Cold War, the United States viewed Israel as a strategic ally in the Middle East, which further solidified its support. The Soviet Union, on the other hand, backed Arab nations, leading to a power struggle in the region and exacerbating the conflict.

The role of Palestinian nationalism cannot be overlooked when discussing the United States' support for Israel. The United States, while recognizing the rights of Palestinians, has consistently favored Israel in its policies due to its close ties with the Jewish state. This has contributed to the perpetuation of the conflict and the marginalization of Palestinian aspirations.

The impact of the Israeli settlement movement and the territorial disputes and border conflicts have further complicated the conflict. The United States' support for Israel has often been criticized for enabling the expansion of settlements and hindering the peace process.

In terms of international organizations, the United States has historically used its veto power in the United Nations Security Council to protect Israel from international condemnation. This has been a contentious issue, as it has hindered efforts to resolve the conflict through diplomatic means.

The Camp David Accords, signed in 1978 between Israel and Egypt, marked a significant milestone in the Arab-Israeli conflict. The United States played a crucial role in brokering the peace agreement, which led to the return of the Sinai Peninsula to Egypt. However, the impact of the accords on the broader conflict has been limited.

Lastly, the influence of terrorism and guerrilla warfare cannot be ignored. The United States has condemned acts of terrorism targeting Israel, further strengthening its support for the Jewish state.

In conclusion, the United States' support for Israel in the Arab-Israeli conflict can be attributed to a combination of historical, religious, geopolitical, and strategic factors. While this support has been instrumental in the survival and development of Israel, it has also contributed to the perpetuation of the conflict and the marginalization of Palestinian aspirations. Understanding the dynamics of this support is crucial for historians studying the Arab-Israeli conflict.

Soviet Union's Involvement in the Conflict

The Arab-Israeli conflict, a complex and multifaceted struggle, has been influenced by a multitude of external powers throughout its history. One of the most influential actors in this conflict was the Soviet Union. From the early days of the conflict to the Cold War era, the Soviet Union played a significant role in shaping the dynamics and outcomes of the Arab-Israeli conflict.

The Soviet Union's involvement in the conflict can be traced back to its ideological and geopolitical interests. As a communist state, the Soviet Union saw an opportunity to expand its influence in the Middle East by supporting Arab states against Israel. The Soviet Union's support for the Arabs was also driven by its desire to counter the influence of the United States, which had traditionally aligned itself with Israel.

One of the key ways in which the Soviet Union supported Arab states was through the provision of military and economic aid. The Soviet Union supplied Arab countries with weapons, military equipment, and training, which significantly bolstered their military capabilities. This support allowed Arab states to challenge Israel's military superiority and escalate the conflict.

Furthermore, the Soviet Union played a crucial role in championing the Palestinian cause and promoting Palestinian nationalism. The Soviet Union recognized the Palestinian Liberation Organization (PLO) as the legitimate representative of the Palestinian people and provided them with political and diplomatic support. The Soviet Union's backing of the PLO helped elevate the Palestinian cause on the international stage and gave legitimacy to their struggle against Israeli occupation.

In addition to its support for Arab states and the Palestinians, the Soviet Union also played a significant role in international organizations involved in resolving the conflict. The Soviet Union used its veto power in the United Nations Security Council to protect Arab interests and thwart resolutions that were unfavorable to their cause. The Soviet Union's influence in the United Nations and the Arab League allowed it to advocate for a more balanced approach to the conflict and challenge the dominance of Western powers.

However, the Soviet Union's involvement in the conflict waned after the Six-Day War in 1967. The military defeat of Arab states by Israel undermined the credibility of the Soviet Union's support for the Arabs and exposed the limitations of its influence. This shift in dynamics, coupled with the changing geopolitical landscape of the Cold War, led to a gradual decrease in the Soviet Union's involvement in the Arab-Israeli conflict.

In conclusion, the Soviet Union's involvement in the Arab-Israeli conflict was driven by ideological, geopolitical, and strategic considerations. Through military and economic aid, support for Palestinian nationalism, and influence in international organizations, the Soviet Union significantly impacted the dynamics of the conflict. However, its influence waned over time, leading to a reconfiguration of the conflict's power dynamics. Understanding the Soviet Union's involvement is crucial for historians studying the history of the Arab-Israeli conflict and the role of external powers in shaping its trajectory.

Cold War Politics and Proxy Conflicts

During the height of the Cold War, the Arab-Israeli conflict became a battleground for global superpowers, namely the United States and the Soviet Union. This subchapter explores the intricacies of Cold War politics and the proxy conflicts that unfolded in the context of the Arab-Israeli conflict, shedding light on the profound impact these external powers had on the region.

The influence of the United States and the Soviet Union on the Arab-Israeli conflict cannot be underestimated. Both powers sought to gain strategic advantages and expand their spheres of influence in the Middle East. The United States, in particular, supported Israel as a key ally in the region, providing military aid and diplomatic backing. On the other hand, the Soviet Union aligned itself with Arab countries, such as Egypt and Syria, offering military equipment and political support.

The Cold War dynamics exacerbated the existing religious and cultural differences between Israelis and Arabs. This subchapter delves into the role of these differences in fueling the conflict, as well as the impact of British colonialism on the Arab-Israeli conflict. The legacy of colonialism, with its arbitrary borders and divide-and-rule policies, further deepened the grievances and tensions between the two sides.

Moreover, the rise of Palestinian nationalism played a crucial role in shaping the Arab-Israeli conflict. This subchapter explores how Palestinian nationalism emerged as a potent force and how it influenced the conflict's dynamics, including the rise of terrorism and guerrilla warfare as tactics employed by Palestinian groups.

The territorial disputes and border conflicts in the Arab-Israeli conflict are also examined, shedding light on the complexities of the conflict's geography. The impact of the Israeli settlement movement, which sought to establish Jewish settlements in the occupied territories, is analyzed in the context of its effect on the conflict.

Furthermore, this subchapter delves into the role of international organizations, such as the United Nations and the Arab League, in attempting to resolve the Arab-Israeli conflict. It also examines the impact of landmark events like the Six-Day War and the Camp David Accords on the conflict dynamics.

In conclusion, this subchapter on Cold War Politics and Proxy Conflicts provides a comprehensive analysis of the external powers' influence on the Arab-Israeli conflict. It explores the historical and geopolitical context, shedding light on the various factors that contributed to the enduring nature of the conflict. Historians and enthusiasts of the history of the Arab-Israeli conflict will find this subchapter invaluable in understanding the complex dynamics that shaped the region during the Cold War era.

International Diplomacy and Peace Initiatives

International diplomacy and peace initiatives have played a crucial role in shaping the Arab-Israeli conflict throughout its history. This subchapter explores the various efforts made by different actors to achieve peace and resolve the complex issues at the heart of this conflict. From the Balfour Declaration to the Oslo Accords, this section delves into the impact of international players, the consequences of colonialism, religious and cultural differences, and the role of nationalism in shaping the conflict.

One of the key aspects that historians explore in this subchapter is the impact of British colonialism on the Arab-Israeli conflict. The British Empire's involvement in the region, particularly after the Balfour Declaration in 1917, significantly influenced the dynamics of the conflict. The establishment of a Jewish homeland in Palestine led to a series of events that continue to shape the conflict to this day.

Additionally, the role of religious and cultural differences cannot be ignored when examining the Arab-Israeli conflict. The clash between Zionism and Palestinian nationalism, rooted in religious and cultural disparities, has perpetuated tensions and hindered the peace process.

Historians delve into the historical context of these differences and their impact on the conflict.

Furthermore, the influence of external powers, such as the United States and the Soviet Union, is examined in relation to their involvement in the Arab-Israeli conflict. These superpowers have historically supported different actors in the region, which has had a significant impact on the conflict's trajectory.

Palestinian nationalism is another critical factor explored in this subchapter. Historians analyze the rise of Palestinian nationalism and its role in the conflict, as well as the various movements and organizations that have emerged to fight for Palestinian rights.

Territorial disputes and border conflicts are also examined in this section, as they have been a recurring issue in the Arab-Israeli conflict. Historians delve into the historical origins of these disputes and their impact on the conflict's escalation.

Moreover, the subchapter delves into the role of international organizations, such as the United Nations and the Arab League, in resolving the conflict. Their efforts to mediate and facilitate peace negotiations, as well as their impact on the conflict's resolution, are thoroughly explored.

The impact of landmark events, such as the Camp David Accords and the Six-Day War, is also analyzed in this subchapter. These events had far-reaching consequences on the conflict's dynamics and the prospects for peace.

Lastly, the subchapter addresses the influence of terrorism and guerrilla warfare in the Arab-Israeli conflict. Historians examine the use of these tactics by different actors and their impact on the conflict's development.

In conclusion, this subchapter provides historians with a comprehensive analysis of international diplomacy and peace initiatives in the Arab-Israeli conflict. It covers a wide range of topics, including the role of external powers, the impact of colonialism, religious and cultural differences, Palestinian nationalism, territorial disputes, landmark events, and the influence of terrorism. By examining these aspects, historians gain a deeper understanding of the complexities and challenges involved in resolving this long-standing conflict.

Chapter 5: The Role of Palestinian Nationalism in the Arab-Israeli Conflict

Emergence of Palestinian National Identity

The Emergence of Palestinian National Identity

The emergence of Palestinian national identity is a crucial aspect in understanding the complexities of the Arab-Israeli conflict. This subchapter explores the historical development of Palestinian nationalism and its impact on the conflict. It delves into the various factors that contributed to the formation of a distinct Palestinian identity, including the influence of British colonialism, religious and cultural differences, external powers, and the role of international organizations.

British colonialism played a significant role in shaping the Arab-Israeli conflict, and the emergence of Palestinian national identity cannot be understood without considering its impact. The British mandate in Palestine from 1920 to 1948 greatly affected the Palestinian population, as it fueled Arab resentment towards Zionist settlement and Jewish immigration. The policies of the British administration, such as the 1939 White Paper, which restricted Jewish immigration, contributed to the growing sense of Palestinian national consciousness.

Religious and cultural differences also played a crucial role in the development of Palestinian national identity. The Palestinians, predominantly Arab Muslims, shared a common language, history, and cultural heritage, which fostered a sense of unity and identity. The attachment to the land, particularly Jerusalem, as a religious and cultural symbol, further strengthened their national identity.

The influence of external powers on the Arab-Israeli conflict, such as the United States and the Soviet Union, also shaped Palestinian national identity. These powers provided political, military, and financial support to various factions within the Palestinian nationalist movement, further solidifying their identity as a distinct national group.

International organizations, particularly the United Nations and the Arab League, played a significant role in shaping Palestinian national identity. The United Nations Partition Plan of 1947, which proposed the division of Palestine into separate Jewish and Arab states, was a pivotal moment in the formation of Palestinian national consciousness. The rejection of this plan by Arab states and Palestinians further solidified their sense of unity and determination.

In conclusion, the emergence of Palestinian national identity is a complex and multifaceted process that cannot be attributed to a single factor. It is a result of various historical, political, and cultural influences. Understanding the development of Palestinian nationalism is crucial in comprehending the intricacies of the Arab-Israeli conflict and the ongoing struggle for self-determination and statehood.

Palestinian Leadership and Resistance Movements

The Palestinian leadership and resistance movements have played a crucial role in shaping the Arab-Israeli conflict throughout history. From the early days of British colonialism to the present day, these groups have been at the forefront of Palestinian nationalist aspirations and the struggle for self-determination.

Under British colonial rule, Palestinian leadership emerged in various forms. The Arab Higher Committee, led by Haj Amin al-Husseini, sought to mobilize Palestinian opposition to Zionist immigration and land acquisition. However, the British mandate also witnessed the

emergence of armed resistance movements, such as the Haganah and
Irgun, among Zionist groups.

The influence of religious and cultural differences cannot be
overlooked in understanding the Arab-Israeli conflict. The conflict has
deep roots in the competing claims of Jews and Arabs to the land of
historical Palestine, which is considered sacred by both religions. These
differences have fueled tensions and served as rallying points for both
sides.

External powers have exerted significant influence on the conflict. The
United States, for instance, has been a staunch supporter of Israel,
providing military aid and diplomatic backing. The Soviet Union, on
the other hand, supported Arab states and Palestinian factions,
contributing to the ongoing dynamic of external involvement and
geopolitical rivalries in the region.

Palestinian nationalism has been a driving force behind the conflict.
The Palestinian Liberation Organization (PLO), founded in 1964,
sought to represent the aspirations of the Palestinian people and their
desire for an independent state. The PLO, led by iconic figures such as
Yasser Arafat, employed various strategies, including armed resistance
and diplomatic efforts, to achieve their goals.

The Israeli settlement movement has had a profound impact on the
Arab-Israeli conflict. The establishment and expansion of Israeli
settlements in the occupied territories have been a major source of
contention, undermining the prospects for a two-state solution and
exacerbating tensions on the ground.

Territorial disputes and border conflicts have been recurring issues in
the Arab-Israeli conflict. The 1948 Arab-Israeli War, the Six-Day War
in 1967, and the Yom Kippur War in 1973 all resulted in changes to

borders and territorial control, further complicating the conflict and contributing to ongoing hostilities.

International organizations, such as the United Nations and the Arab League, have played a role in attempting to resolve the conflict. However, their efforts have often been hampered by divisions among member states and the influence of external powers.

The Camp David Accords of 1978 had a significant impact on the conflict, as it paved the way for the peace treaty between Israel and Egypt. While it marked an important milestone, the unresolved Palestinian question remained a major obstacle to a comprehensive and lasting peace.

Terrorism and guerrilla warfare have also left an indelible mark on the Arab-Israeli conflict. From the actions of groups like Hamas and Islamic Jihad to the activities of the PLO, these tactics have been employed by various factions in their struggle against Israeli occupation.

In conclusion, understanding the role of Palestinian leadership and resistance movements is essential to comprehending the complexities of the Arab-Israeli conflict. From the impact of British colonialism to the influence of external powers and the dynamics of religious and cultural differences, these factors have shaped the conflict's trajectory and continue to impact its resolution. The struggle for Palestinian self-determination remains a central issue, and the actions of both Palestinian leaders and resistance groups have played a crucial role in shaping the conflict's narrative throughout history.

Intifadas and Popular Uprisings

Intifadas and Popular Uprisings: A Turning Point in the Arab-Israeli Conflict

The subchapter "Intifadas and Popular Uprisings" delves into a significant turning point in the Arab-Israeli conflict. Historians studying the history of this conflict, the impact of British colonialism, the role of religious and cultural differences, the influence of external powers, and the role of Palestinian nationalism will find this chapter particularly engaging.

The Intifadas, meaning "uprisings" in Arabic, refer to two major waves of popular resistance against Israeli occupation in the Palestinian territories. The First Intifada erupted in 1987 and lasted until 1993, while the Second Intifada began in 2000 and continued for several years. These uprisings marked a shift in Palestinian resistance tactics and had a profound impact on the Arab-Israeli conflict.

One of the key factors leading to the Intifadas was the frustration and despair felt by Palestinians living under Israeli occupation. The Intifadas were spontaneous and grassroots movements, driven by a sense of injustice and a desire for self-determination. Young Palestinians, often armed only with stones, took to the streets to protest against Israeli policies and demand their rights.

The Intifadas also highlighted the power of collective action and civil disobedience. Palestinians employed a range of tactics, including strikes, boycotts, and demonstrations, to challenge Israeli control. These uprisings attracted international attention and support, shining a spotlight on the Palestinian struggle for statehood and drawing sympathy from around the world.

The Israeli response to the Intifadas was harsh and controversial. The Israeli military cracked down on the uprisings, employing heavy-handed tactics that led to significant casualties and human rights abuses. These actions further fueled Palestinian resentment and solidified international criticism of Israeli policies.

The Intifadas also had a lasting impact on the Arab-Israeli conflict. They demonstrated that Palestinians were not passive victims but active agents in their struggle for independence. The uprisings forced Israelis to confront the realities of occupation and raised questions about the viability of a two-state solution.

Furthermore, the Intifadas influenced the international perception of the conflict. They brought attention to the plight of the Palestinians and increased pressure on the international community to find a resolution. The United Nations, Arab League, and other international organizations played a vital role in mediating the conflict and pushing for a peaceful settlement.

Lastly, the Intifadas also witnessed a rise in terrorism and guerrilla warfare as Palestinians sought alternative means to resist Israeli occupation. While these tactics were controversial, they further complicated efforts to find a peaceful resolution to the conflict.

In conclusion, the Intifadas and popular uprisings were pivotal moments in the Arab-Israeli conflict. They highlighted the power of grassroots resistance, brought attention to the Palestinian struggle for self-determination, and influenced international perceptions of the conflict. Historians examining the history of the Arab-Israeli conflict and its various dimensions will find the Intifadas and popular uprisings to be a fascinating and important topic of study.

Negotiations and Challenges to Palestinian Statehood

The pursuit of Palestinian statehood has been a central aspect of the Arab-Israeli conflict, marked by a complex web of negotiations and challenges. This subchapter delves into the intricate history of the struggle for Palestinian statehood, shedding light on the key events, actors, and dynamics that have shaped this ongoing conflict.

From the early 20th century, the impact of British colonialism on the Arab-Israeli conflict cannot be overstated. The Balfour Declaration of 1917, in which Britain expressed support for the establishment of a Jewish homeland in Palestine, set the stage for decades of tension and competing national aspirations. The clash between Jewish Zionist aspirations and Palestinian nationalism fueled the conflict, with religious and cultural differences exacerbating the divide.

External powers have played a significant role in the Arab-Israeli conflict, particularly the United States and the Soviet Union. These superpowers often aligned with one side or the other, wielding influence through diplomatic, military, and economic means. Their interventions have shaped the trajectory of negotiations and have sometimes hindered progress towards a resolution.

Palestinian nationalism emerged as a powerful force in the conflict, manifesting in various political and armed movements. From the Palestinian Liberation Organization (PLO) to Hamas, these groups have sought to advance Palestinian self-determination and statehood through a multitude of strategies, including diplomacy, terrorism, and guerrilla warfare.

The Israeli settlement movement has had a profound impact on the Arab-Israeli conflict. The expansion of Israeli settlements in the occupied territories has not only created territorial disputes and border conflicts but has also posed significant challenges to the viability of a future Palestinian state. The establishment of settlements has been a contentious issue in negotiations and has often been met with international condemnation.

The Six-Day War of 1967 marked a pivotal moment in the Arab-Israeli conflict. Israel's swift military victory led to the occupation of the West Bank, Gaza Strip, and East Jerusalem, setting the stage for prolonged territorial disputes and deepening Palestinian grievances.

International organizations, such as the United Nations and the Arab League, have sought to mediate and resolve the conflict. Their efforts, including numerous resolutions, peace plans, and diplomatic initiatives, have had varying degrees of success in bridging the gaps between the parties involved.

The Camp David Accords of 1978 brought about a historic peace agreement between Israel and Egypt, but its impact on the broader Arab-Israeli conflict remains a subject of debate. While the accords addressed the issue of Israeli-Egyptian relations, they did not fully address the core issues of Palestinian statehood, leaving them unresolved.

Throughout the history of the conflict, terrorism and guerrilla warfare have played a significant role. From the attacks carried out by Palestinian groups to Israeli military operations, these violent tactics have further deepened the cycle of violence and posed significant challenges to achieving a peaceful resolution.

In conclusion, the subchapter on negotiations and challenges to Palestinian statehood in "From Balfour to Oslo: A Comprehensive History of the Arab-Israeli Conflict" explores the multifaceted dimensions of this protracted struggle. By examining the impact of British colonialism, the role of religious and cultural differences, the influence of external powers, the significance of Palestinian nationalism, the implications of Israeli settlements, the territorial disputes and border conflicts, the consequences of the Six-Day War, the efforts of international organizations, the impact of the Camp David Accords, and the role of terrorism and guerrilla warfare, historians gain a comprehensive understanding of the complexities that continue to shape the Arab-Israeli conflict.

Chapter 6: The Impact of the Israeli Settlement Movement on the Arab-Israeli Conflict

Settlement Expansion and Land Disputes

Settlement expansion and land disputes have been central to the long-standing Arab-Israeli conflict, shaping its trajectory and exacerbating tensions between the two sides. This subchapter will delve into the historical background and impact of settlement expansion, highlighting its implications for territorial disputes and border conflicts. Additionally, it will address the role of external powers, particularly the United States and the Soviet Union, in influencing settlement policies and exacerbating land disputes.

The roots of settlement expansion lie in the Zionist movement's aspiration to establish a Jewish homeland in Palestine. Following the Balfour Declaration in 1917, which expressed British support for a Jewish homeland, Jewish immigration to Palestine increased significantly. This influx of Jewish settlers led to land disputes with the Arab population, as Palestinians viewed their presence as an encroachment on their ancestral lands.

British colonialism further complicated the issue. The British Mandatory authorities implemented policies favoring Jewish settlement, often disregarding the concerns of the Arab majority. These policies, combined with the influx of Jewish immigrants fleeing persecution, fueled tensions and land disputes between the Jewish and Arab communities.

The establishment of the State of Israel in 1948 marked a turning point in settlement expansion. Israel's victory in the 1948 Arab-Israeli War resulted in an influx of Jewish refugees and the displacement of

Palestinian Arabs. This displacement created a significant land void, which the Israeli government sought to fill through the establishment of new settlements. The Israeli settlement movement gained momentum in the following decades, as successive Israeli governments encouraged Jewish settlers to establish communities in the occupied territories, particularly the West Bank and Gaza Strip.

The impact of settlement expansion on the Arab-Israeli conflict cannot be understated. The establishment of Israeli settlements has resulted in the dispossession and displacement of Palestinians, leading to a deep sense of resentment and fueling Palestinian nationalism. The expansion of settlements has also complicated attempts to resolve territorial disputes and border conflicts, as Israeli settlements often encroach upon land claimed by Palestinians for a future state.

External powers have played a pivotal role in influencing settlement policies and exacerbating land disputes. The United States, through its financial and diplomatic support for Israel, has been a key enabler of settlement expansion. The Soviet Union, on the other hand, aligned itself with Arab states and supported their opposition to Israeli settlements. The involvement of these external powers has complicated efforts to find a peaceful resolution to the conflict and has perpetuated the cycle of land disputes.

In conclusion, settlement expansion and land disputes have been central to the Arab-Israeli conflict. The establishment and expansion of Israeli settlements have fueled tensions, contributed to territorial disputes, and exacerbated the conflict. The influence of external powers in shaping settlement policies has further complicated the issue. Understanding the historical background and impact of settlement expansion is crucial in comprehending the complexities of the Arab-Israeli conflict and exploring potential avenues for resolution.

Israeli Government Policies and Settlement Construction

The Israeli Government's policies and settlement construction have played a significant role in shaping the Arab-Israeli conflict throughout history. These policies have been influenced by a multitude of factors, including the impact of British colonialism, religious and cultural differences, external powers, Palestinian nationalism, territorial disputes, and border conflicts.

One of the key factors in understanding Israeli government policies and settlement construction is the impact of British colonialism. The Balfour Declaration of 1917, issued by the British government, expressed support for the establishment of a Jewish homeland in Palestine. This declaration laid the foundation for future Israeli policies and settlement construction, as it provided a legal and diplomatic basis for Jewish migration to the region.

Religious and cultural differences have also played a crucial role in the conflict. The Israeli government's policies have often been driven by the desire to protect and promote Jewish interests, while the Palestinian population has sought to preserve their own cultural and religious heritage. These differing perspectives have fueled tensions and led to the establishment of settlements in disputed territories.

External powers, such as the United States and the Soviet Union, have also exerted influence on Israeli government policies. These powers have often provided political, economic, and military support to Israel, which has enabled the government to advance its settlement construction agenda. Conversely, external powers have also played a role in supporting the Palestinian cause and advocating for a resolution to the conflict.

The Israeli settlement movement, which involves the construction of Jewish communities in the occupied territories, has had a significant impact on the Arab-Israeli conflict. These settlements have often been viewed as illegal under international law and have been a major source of contention between Israelis and Palestinians. The Israeli government's policies of settlement construction have contributed to the expansion of Israeli control over disputed territories, further complicating efforts to reach a peaceful resolution.

Territorial disputes and border conflicts have been a consistent feature of the Arab-Israeli conflict, and Israeli government policies have played a significant role in exacerbating these tensions. The Six-Day War of 1967, for example, resulted in Israel gaining control over the West Bank, Gaza Strip, and East Jerusalem. The Israeli government's subsequent establishment of settlements in these areas has been a major source of contention and has hindered peace negotiations.

The role of international organizations, such as the United Nations and the Arab League, in resolving the Arab-Israeli conflict has been crucial. These organizations have sought to mediate negotiations, promote peace initiatives, and address the issue of Israeli settlements. However, their efforts have often been hampered by the complexities of the conflict and the differing interests of the parties involved.

The impact of the Camp David Accords in 1978, which resulted in a peace treaty between Israel and Egypt, cannot be understated. This agreement marked a significant turning point in the conflict and demonstrated the potential for peaceful resolution. However, the issue of Israeli settlement construction has remained a major obstacle to further progress.

Finally, the influence of terrorism and guerrilla warfare has also shaped the Arab-Israeli conflict. Acts of violence committed by both Israelis and Palestinians have further deepened mistrust and hindered peace negotiations. Israeli government policies, particularly those related to settlement construction, have been a contributing factor in fueling this cycle of violence.

In conclusion, the Israeli government's policies and settlement construction have had a profound impact on the Arab-Israeli conflict. These policies have been influenced by a range of factors, including British colonialism, religious and cultural differences, external powers, Palestinian nationalism, territorial disputes, and border conflicts. Understanding these dynamics is crucial for historians studying the history of the Arab-Israeli conflict and its ongoing implications.

International Reactions and Legal Implications

The Arab-Israeli conflict has been a subject of intense interest and concern for the international community. The conflict, rooted in a complex web of historical, religious, and political factors, has elicited various reactions from nations around the world, with significant legal implications.

From its inception, the conflict attracted the attention of external powers, most notably the United States and the Soviet Union. These superpowers saw the Arab-Israeli conflict as a strategic opportunity to advance their own interests in the region. The United States, in particular, has played a pivotal role in mediating peace negotiations and providing military aid to Israel. The Soviet Union, on the other hand, supported Arab nations, providing them with arms and diplomatic support.

The conflict also drew the attention of international organizations, such as the United Nations and the Arab League. The United Nations, through numerous resolutions, attempted to address the territorial disputes and border conflicts between Israel and its Arab neighbors. However, these resolutions have often been met with resistance and non-compliance from both sides, further complicating the conflict.

One of the most significant international reactions to the Arab-Israeli conflict was the Camp David Accords in 1978. These accords, brokered by the United States, brought about a historic peace agreement between Egypt and Israel. Although the accords did not resolve all the issues in the conflict, they marked a significant step towards peace and had a lasting impact on the region.

The conflict has also been marred by acts of terrorism and guerrilla warfare, with various Palestinian groups resorting to violence as a means to advance their cause. These acts of terrorism have not only further escalated the conflict but have also raised important legal questions regarding the use of force and the rights of civilians.

Moreover, the impact of the Israeli settlement movement on the Arab-Israeli conflict cannot be understated. The establishment of Israeli settlements in the occupied territories has been a major source of contention and has been widely criticized by the international community for its violation of international law.

The Arab-Israeli conflict is a multifaceted issue that has been shaped by numerous historical, political, and legal factors. Its international reactions and legal implications have played a significant role in shaping the dynamics of the conflict. Understanding these complexities is crucial for historians studying the history of the Arab-Israeli conflict and its various interconnected themes.

Settler Violence and Palestinian Displacement

The subchapter "Settler Violence and Palestinian Displacement" explores a critical aspect of the Arab-Israeli conflict, shedding light on the impact of Israeli settlements on the Palestinian population. This topic is of utmost importance to historians studying the conflict's history and its various dimensions, including the role of external powers, territorial disputes, and the influence of religious and cultural differences.

The establishment of Israeli settlements in the occupied territories has been a central aspect of the conflict and has led to numerous incidents of settler violence. These settlements, constructed primarily by Israeli civilians in the West Bank and East Jerusalem, have been a source of tension and conflict between Israelis and Palestinians. Historians studying the Arab-Israeli conflict recognize the significance of settler violence as a catalyst for Palestinian displacement.

The settlements have been a major obstacle to peace negotiations, as they have encroached upon Palestinian land, disrupted communities, and often led to violent clashes. Palestinian displacement has been a direct consequence of these settlements, with Palestinians being forced from their homes and land to make way for Israeli settlers. This displacement has resulted in a profound humanitarian crisis, with thousands of Palestinians losing their homes and becoming refugees in their own land.

Historians examining the Arab-Israeli conflict also analyze the role of international organizations, such as the United Nations and the Arab League, in addressing the issue of settlements and the resulting displacement. These organizations have played a significant role in condemning Israeli settlement activities and advocating for the rights of Palestinians affected by the settlements.

Furthermore, the subchapter explores the impact of the Israeli settlement movement on the conflict as a whole. Settlement expansion has not only led to Palestinian displacement but has also complicated the issue of territorial disputes and border conflicts. The settlements have been a major point of contention in negotiations and have hindered the possibility of a two-state solution.

Overall, the subchapter on "Settler Violence and Palestinian Displacement" provides historians with a comprehensive understanding of the complex dynamics surrounding Israeli settlements and their role in the Arab-Israeli conflict. It highlights the devastating consequences of settler violence on the Palestinian population, the obstacles it poses to peace negotiations, and the role of international organizations in addressing these issues. This analysis brings historians closer to comprehending the complexities of the conflict and its multifaceted dimensions.

Chapter 7: Territorial Disputes and Border Conflicts in the Arab-Israeli Conflict

Partition Plans and Border Demarcations

In the tumultuous history of the Arab-Israeli conflict, partition plans and border demarcations have played a pivotal role in shaping the ongoing struggle between the two nations. This subchapter explores the various attempts to divide the land and establish borders that have both united and further divided the parties involved.

One of the earliest and most significant partition plans was the Balfour Declaration of 1917, which expressed British support for the establishment of a national home for the Jewish people in Palestine. This declaration laid the groundwork for future partition plans, as it recognized the aspirations of both the Jewish and Arab populations in the region. However, it also sowed the seeds for conflict, as it failed to address the concerns and rights of the Arab majority.

In 1947, the United Nations proposed a partition plan to resolve the escalating tensions between Jewish and Arab communities in Palestine. This plan recommended the division of Palestine into separate Jewish and Arab states, with Jerusalem placed under international administration. While accepted by the Jewish leadership, the plan was vehemently rejected by the Arab states, leading to the 1948 Arab-Israeli War.

The aftermath of this war saw significant border demarcations, as armistice lines were drawn between Israel and its neighboring Arab states. These lines, known as the Green Line, served as de facto borders until the Six-Day War of 1967, when Israel occupied the West Bank, Gaza Strip, and East Jerusalem. This occupation not only further complicated the territorial disputes but also intensified the Arab-Israeli conflict.

Throughout the conflict, external powers have played a crucial role in influencing the outcomes of partition plans and border demarcations. The United States, for instance, has been a staunch supporter of Israel, providing military aid and diplomatic support. The Soviet Union also played a significant role, initially supporting the Arab states but later aligning itself with Israel's enemies.

The Arab-Israeli conflict has been deeply influenced by religious and cultural differences, as both sides claim historical and religious ties to the land. Palestinian nationalism, fueled by a desire for self-determination and statehood, has also been a driving force in the conflict.

International organizations such as the United Nations and Arab League have attempted to mediate and resolve the conflict through various initiatives and resolutions. The Camp David Accords of 1978 marked a significant milestone in the peace process, as it led to the signing of a peace treaty between Israel and Egypt, the first Arab state to formally recognize Israel.

The impact of the Israeli settlement movement and the use of terrorism and guerrilla warfare tactics by both sides have further complicated the territorial disputes and border conflicts.

In conclusion, partition plans and border demarcations have been central to the Arab-Israeli conflict, shaping its trajectory and intensifying the struggle between the parties involved. The influence of external powers, the role of religious and cultural differences, and the aspirations of Palestinian nationalism have all contributed to the complexity of this long-standing conflict. While efforts have been made by international organizations and through peace agreements, the resolution of the Arab-Israeli conflict remains an ongoing challenge.

Wars and Military Actions

The Arab-Israeli conflict has been marked by numerous wars and military actions that have shaped the course of history in the region. From the early stages of British colonialism to the present day, these events have had a profound impact on the conflict and its various dimensions.

British colonialism played a significant role in the Arab-Israeli conflict. The Balfour Declaration of 1917, which promised British support for a "national home for the Jewish people" in Palestine, laid the groundwork for the establishment of Israel and ignited tensions between Jewish and Arab communities. The subsequent British mandate in Palestine further fueled these tensions, leading to armed resistance and uprisings.

Religious and cultural differences have also played a crucial role in the conflict. The dispute over the control of Jerusalem, a city sacred to both Jews and Muslims, has been a major source of contention. The conflicting religious narratives and deep-rooted cultural identities have contributed to the intractability of the conflict and hindered peaceful resolution.

External powers, particularly the United States and the Soviet Union, have exerted significant influence over the Arab-Israeli conflict. The Cold War rivalry between these superpowers further complicated the dynamics of the conflict, with each side supporting different factions and perpetuating the cycle of violence.

Palestinian nationalism has been a driving force in the Arab-Israeli conflict. The struggle for self-determination and the establishment of a Palestinian state has mobilized generations of Palestinians, leading to various forms of resistance and armed struggle against Israeli occupation.

The Israeli settlement movement has also played a crucial role in shaping the conflict. The establishment of Israeli settlements in the occupied territories has been a major point of contention, fueling tensions and undermining prospects for peace.

Territorial disputes and border conflicts have been recurring themes in the Arab-Israeli conflict. The contested borders, particularly in the West Bank and Gaza Strip, have been a source of frequent clashes and military actions.

The Six-Day War of 1967 had a profound impact on the Arab-Israeli conflict. Israel's stunning victory and its subsequent occupation of the West Bank, Gaza Strip, and East Jerusalem fundamentally altered the dynamics of the conflict, leading to increased Palestinian resistance and setting the stage for further conflicts.

International organizations, such as the United Nations and the Arab League, have played a role in attempting to resolve the conflict. However, their efforts have often been hindered by political divisions and competing interests, preventing a comprehensive and lasting resolution.

The Camp David Accords of 1978 marked a significant turning point in the conflict. The peace agreement between Israel and Egypt, brokered by the United States, paved the way for diplomatic relations between the two countries and highlighted the potential for peaceful resolutions.

Terrorism and guerrilla warfare have also been influential factors in the Arab-Israeli conflict. Acts of violence perpetrated by both sides have further escalated tensions and perpetuated a cycle of revenge and retaliation.

In conclusion, the Arab-Israeli conflict has been shaped by a series of wars and military actions, influenced by British colonialism, religious and cultural differences, external powers, Palestinian nationalism, the Israeli settlement movement, territorial disputes, and the impact of significant events such as the Six-Day War and the Camp David Accords. Understanding these historical aspects is crucial for historians studying the complex dynamics of the conflict and its potential for resolution.

Occupation and Annexation

In the complex tapestry of the Arab-Israeli conflict, the issue of occupation and annexation has played a central role. This subchapter delves into the historical context, the impact of British colonialism, the role of religious and cultural differences, the influence of external powers, the role of Palestinian nationalism, territorial disputes and border conflicts, the impact of the Six-Day War, the role of international organizations, the Camp David Accords, and the influence of terrorism and guerrilla warfare.

Occupation and annexation have been critical components of the Arab-Israeli conflict, shaping the course of events and the dynamics between the parties involved. The roots of this conflict can be traced back to the era of British colonialism, which shaped the political landscape of the region. The impact of British colonialism on the Arab-Israeli conflict cannot be overstated, as it led to the establishment of a Jewish homeland in Palestine and the subsequent displacement and dispossession of Palestinians.

Religious and cultural differences have also played a significant role in fueling the conflict. The deep-seated religious and cultural roots of both Israelis and Palestinians have fueled the sense of identity and the desire for self-determination. These differences have often been exploited by external powers, such as the United States and the Soviet Union, who have played influential roles in shaping the conflict.

The rise of Palestinian nationalism has been a significant factor in the Arab-Israeli conflict. The Palestinian people have fought for their right to self-determination and have engaged in various forms of resistance against Israeli occupation and annexation. The Israeli settlement movement, which involves the establishment of Jewish settlements in occupied territories, has further complicated the situation, sparking territorial disputes and border conflicts.

The Six-Day War in 1967 had a profound impact on the Arab-Israeli conflict. Israel's swift victory resulted in the occupation of the West Bank, Gaza Strip, and East Jerusalem, further exacerbating tensions and territorial disputes. International organizations, such as the United Nations and the Arab League, have played important roles in attempting to resolve the conflict, although their efforts have often been hampered by political complexities and competing interests.

The Camp David Accords in 1978 marked a significant milestone in the Arab-Israeli conflict, as it led to a peace treaty between Israel and Egypt. However, the accords did not address the core issues of the conflict, and the conflict continued to simmer, leading to further violence and unrest.

Terrorism and guerrilla warfare have also played a significant role in the Arab-Israeli conflict. Various extremist groups have resorted to violent means in their struggle for self-determination, further complicating the path to peace.

In conclusion, the issue of occupation and annexation has been a central theme in the Arab-Israeli conflict. Understanding the historical context, the impact of British colonialism, the role of religious and cultural differences, the influence of external powers, the role of

Palestinian nationalism, territorial disputes and border conflicts, the impact of the Six-Day War, the role of international organizations, the Camp David Accords, and the influence of terrorism and guerrilla warfare is essential for historians seeking a comprehensive understanding of this complex conflict.

Gaza Strip and West Bank: The Two-State Solution Debate

The Gaza Strip and West Bank have been at the center of the Arab-Israeli conflict for decades. The question of how to resolve the territorial disputes and achieve a lasting peace between Israelis and Palestinians has been the subject of intense debate. One proposed solution that has gained significant attention is the two-state solution.

The two-state solution envisions the establishment of an independent Palestinian state alongside Israel, with the Gaza Strip and West Bank as its territories. Advocates argue that this approach would allow both Israelis and Palestinians to have their own self-determination and fulfill their national aspirations. Proponents believe that the creation of two separate states would enable the two peoples to live side by side in peace, with mutually recognized and secure borders.

However, the two-state solution is not without its challenges and controversies. Critics argue that the Israeli settlement movement, which involves the construction of Israeli communities in the occupied territories, poses a significant obstacle to the establishment of a viable Palestinian state. These settlements have expanded over the years, leading to the displacement of Palestinian communities and the fragmentation of the West Bank.

Religious and cultural differences also play a crucial role in the debate. The holy sites of Jerusalem, which are of great significance to both Jews and Muslims, have been a major point of contention. The status of

Jerusalem and its division between Israelis and Palestinians remains a contentious issue that has hindered progress in peace negotiations.

External powers, particularly the United States and the Soviet Union during the Cold War, have exerted significant influence on the Arab-Israeli conflict. These powers have provided diplomatic, military, and economic support to their respective allies in the region, shaping the course of the conflict and the prospects for peace.

The role of Palestinian nationalism is another important factor to consider. The Palestinian people have long sought self-determination and statehood, and their nationalist aspirations have played a central role in the conflict. Palestinian resistance movements, including acts of terrorism and guerrilla warfare, have emerged as a response to Israeli occupation and have further complicated efforts to achieve a peaceful resolution.

International organizations, such as the United Nations and the Arab League, have also played a role in attempts to resolve the conflict. The United Nations has passed numerous resolutions calling for a two-state solution and condemning Israeli settlements, while the Arab League has supported the Palestinian cause and advocated for their rights.

The Camp David Accords of 1978, brokered by the United States, marked a significant milestone in the Arab-Israeli conflict. These agreements between Israel and Egypt led to the return of the Sinai Peninsula to Egypt and laid the groundwork for peace between the two countries. However, the accords did not address the larger issues of Palestinian statehood, and the conflict continued.

In conclusion, the two-state solution for the Gaza Strip and West Bank remains a subject of intense debate in the Arab-Israeli conflict. The impact of British colonialism, religious and cultural differences, external powers, Palestinian nationalism, Israeli settlements, territorial disputes, and border conflicts, as well as the role of international organizations, the Six-Day War, the Camp David Accords, and terrorism and guerrilla warfare, have all shaped the discourse surrounding this proposed solution. Historians continue to analyze and assess the various factors that have contributed to the complexity of the conflict and explore potential paths towards a peaceful resolution.

Chapter 8: The Impact of the Six-Day War on the Arab-Israeli Conflict

Causes and Pre-War Tensions

The Arab-Israeli conflict is a complex and multifaceted issue that has its roots in a variety of causes and pre-war tensions. Understanding these factors is essential to comprehending the history of this conflict, which has had a profound impact on the Middle East and international relations.

One significant cause of the Arab-Israeli conflict was the impact of British colonialism on the region. Following World War I, the British Empire gained control over Palestine through the League of Nations' mandate system. This colonial rule created tensions between the indigenous Arab population and Jewish immigrants, who were encouraged by the British government to settle in Palestine under the Balfour Declaration of 1917. These conflicting aspirations for self-determination and competing claims to the land laid the foundation for the conflict.

Religious and cultural differences have also played a vital role in fueling the Arab-Israeli conflict. Jerusalem, a city of great religious significance to Jews, Muslims, and Christians, became a focal point of contention. The competing claims and desires to control religious sites, such as the Western Wall and the Al-Aqsa Mosque, have perpetuated tensions between the two sides.

External powers, particularly the United States and the Soviet Union, have exerted significant influence on the Arab-Israeli conflict. The United States has traditionally supported Israel, providing military aid and political backing, while the Soviet Union aligned itself with Arab states, supplying weapons and diplomatic support. This external involvement has further complicated efforts to achieve peace and has often exacerbated existing tensions.

The rise of Palestinian nationalism has also played a critical role in the Arab-Israeli conflict. The Palestinian people, seeking self-determination and independence, have waged a struggle against Israeli occupation. This nationalist sentiment has been a driving force in the conflict and has shaped the Palestinian resistance movement.

Territorial disputes and border conflicts have been another source of tension in the Arab-Israeli conflict. The establishment of the state of Israel in 1948 led to the displacement of hundreds of thousands of Palestinians and the loss of their land. The subsequent wars, such as the Six-Day War in 1967, further intensified territorial disputes and solidified Israeli control over occupied territories, including the West Bank and Gaza Strip.

International organizations, such as the United Nations and the Arab League, have played a role in attempting to resolve the Arab-Israeli conflict. The United Nations passed numerous resolutions calling for the establishment of a Palestinian state and the withdrawal of Israeli forces from occupied territories. The Arab League has also been involved in diplomatic efforts to address the conflict, advocating for Palestinian rights and supporting Arab states' positions.

Terrorism and guerrilla warfare have had a significant impact on the Arab-Israeli conflict. Both sides have resorted to violence as a means of achieving their goals, leading to numerous acts of terrorism and guerrilla warfare. These tactics have further escalated tensions and hindered efforts to find a peaceful resolution to the conflict.

In conclusion, the causes and pre-war tensions in the Arab-Israeli conflict are numerous and interconnected. British colonialism, religious and cultural differences, external powers' influence,

Palestinian nationalism, territorial disputes, and border conflicts, the impact of the Six-Day War, the role of international organizations, the Camp David Accords, and terrorism have all played crucial roles in shaping the conflict. Understanding these factors is essential for historians studying the history of the Arab-Israeli conflict and its profound impact on the region.

Israeli Military Success and Territory Acquisition

The Israeli military has played a crucial role in shaping the Arab-Israeli conflict and has been instrumental in the acquisition of territory throughout the conflict's history. Understanding the military successes of Israel is essential in comprehending the complex dynamics that have shaped the conflict.

From its inception in 1948, Israel has had to rely heavily on its military to defend its existence and secure its borders. Despite being outnumbered and outgunned by its Arab neighbors, the Israeli military achieved remarkable victories in several key conflicts. One of the most significant military successes was the 1948 Arab-Israeli War, also known as the War of Independence, where Israel successfully defended itself against the invading Arab armies. This victory allowed Israel to consolidate its control over a larger territory than initially envisaged under the United Nations Partition Plan.

In subsequent conflicts, such as the Six-Day War in 1967 and the Yom Kippur War in 1973, the Israeli military's prowess became even more evident. The Six-Day War, in particular, was a decisive victory for Israel, resulting in the capture of the Sinai Peninsula, the West Bank (including East Jerusalem), and the Golan Heights. These territorial acquisitions significantly altered the geopolitical landscape of the region and further intensified the Arab-Israeli conflict.

The Israeli military's success can be attributed to several factors. Firstly, Israel has invested heavily in its military capabilities, particularly in technology and intelligence gathering, allowing it to maintain a qualitative edge over its adversaries. Additionally, Israel's mandatory military service has ensured a large pool of highly trained and motivated soldiers.

Furthermore, the Israeli military has benefitted from the unwavering support of external powers, most notably the United States. The U.S. has provided Israel with substantial military aid and political backing, enabling it to maintain a formidable military force.

However, while Israeli military successes have resulted in territorial gains, they have also contributed to the protracted nature of the conflict. The acquisition of territories, particularly the West Bank and Gaza Strip, has led to ongoing disputes and tensions between Israelis and Palestinians, fueling Palestinian nationalism and resistance movements.

In conclusion, the Israeli military's success and its territorial acquisitions have been pivotal in shaping the Arab-Israeli conflict. Understanding the military dynamics of the conflict is essential for historians studying the complex interplay between military strategy, geopolitics, and the aspirations of different actors involved in the conflict. By examining the Israeli military's achievements and their impact on the conflict, historians can gain valuable insights into the historical context and the ongoing challenges faced in resolving the Arab-Israeli conflict.

Regional and Global Repercussions

The Arab-Israeli conflict is a complex and multifaceted issue that has had far-reaching regional and global repercussions throughout its history. This subchapter will explore the various aspects that have shaped and influenced the conflict, shedding light on its historical context and providing a comprehensive understanding for historians.

One of the key factors that has influenced the Arab-Israeli conflict is the impact of British colonialism. The British Mandate in Palestine, established after World War I, played a significant role in shaping the conflict. The Balfour Declaration, issued in 1917, promised British support for the establishment of a Jewish homeland in Palestine. This declaration created tensions between the Jewish and Arab communities, laying the groundwork for future conflicts.

Religious and cultural differences have also played a crucial role in fueling the Arab-Israeli conflict. Both Jews and Arabs have deep historical and religious ties to the land of Palestine, leading to conflicting claims and a sense of entitlement. The clash between Judaism and Islam, further exacerbated by the presence of holy sites such as Jerusalem, has added a religious dimension to the conflict.

External powers, particularly the United States and the Soviet Union, have exerted a significant influence on the Arab-Israeli conflict. Both superpowers had their own geopolitical interests in the region, leading to their involvement and support for different sides. The United States has been a staunch ally of Israel, providing economic and military aid, while the Soviet Union supported Arab nations, particularly during the Cold War era.

Palestinian nationalism has also played a crucial role in the Arab-Israeli conflict. The Palestinian people have long sought self-determination and statehood, leading to the rise of various nationalist movements. The Palestine Liberation Organization (PLO) emerged as a key player, advocating for Palestinian rights and engaging in armed resistance against Israeli occupation.

The Israeli settlement movement, characterized by the establishment of Jewish settlements in occupied territories, has further complicated the conflict. These settlements have been a major source of contention, as they are seen as an obstacle to the establishment of a viable Palestinian state.

Territorial disputes and border conflicts have been a recurring feature of the Arab-Israeli conflict. The status of Jerusalem, the West Bank, Gaza Strip, and the Golan Heights has been a subject of intense debate and negotiation.

The impact of the Six-Day War in 1967 cannot be understated. Israel's stunning military victory resulted in the occupation of more territory and further intensified the conflict, leading to lasting consequences.

International organizations, such as the United Nations and the Arab League, have played a role in attempting to resolve the Arab-Israeli conflict. These organizations have often struggled to find a peaceful resolution due to the complex nature of the conflict and the divergent interests of the parties involved.

The Camp David Accords in 1978 marked a significant milestone in the peace process. The agreement between Israel and Egypt resulted in the first Arab country recognizing Israel's legitimacy. However, it also highlighted the challenges of resolving the conflict and achieving a comprehensive peace agreement.

Lastly, terrorism and guerrilla warfare have had a profound impact on the Arab-Israeli conflict. Acts of violence perpetrated by extremist groups, such as Hamas and Hezbollah, have escalated tensions and hindered the peace process.

In conclusion, the Arab-Israeli conflict has had immense regional and global repercussions. Understanding the historical context, the impact of British colonialism, the role of religious and cultural differences, the influence of external powers, the role of Palestinian nationalism, the impact of the Israeli settlement movement, the territorial disputes, the impact of the Six-Day War, the role of international organizations, the impact of the Camp David Accords, and the influence of terrorism and guerrilla warfare is crucial for historians to grasp the complexities of this enduring conflict.

Post-War Peace Efforts and UN Resolutions

In the aftermath of World War II, the Arab-Israeli conflict entered a new phase, with various post-war peace efforts and United Nations resolutions attempting to address the deep-rooted issues at the heart of the conflict. This subchapter explores the significant developments and initiatives that shaped the conflict during this period.

The impact of British colonialism on the Arab-Israeli conflict cannot be understated. British policies, such as the Balfour Declaration of 1917, laid the groundwork for Jewish immigration to Palestine and fueled Arab resentment. This, coupled with the rise of Palestinian nationalism, resulted in a protracted struggle for self-determination, which significantly influenced the conflict.

External powers, particularly the United States and the Soviet Union, played a pivotal role in the Arab-Israeli conflict. The United States emerged as a staunch ally of Israel, providing military and financial aid, while the Soviet Union supported Arab nations, seeking to gain influence in the region. This Cold War dynamic further intensified the conflict and hindered diplomatic efforts.

The United Nations, as an international organization, actively engaged in resolving the Arab-Israeli conflict through various resolutions. The most notable was the 1947 UN Partition Plan, which recommended the division of Palestine into separate Jewish and Arab states. However, the plan was rejected by Arab nations, leading to the 1948 Arab-Israeli War and further complicating the region's stability.

The Six-Day War of 1967 proved to be a turning point in the conflict. Israel's stunning military victory resulted in the occupation of the West Bank, Gaza Strip, and East Jerusalem. This led to the adoption of UN Security Council Resolution 242, which called for the withdrawal of Israeli forces from occupied territories and a just settlement of the refugee issue.

The Camp David Accords of 1978 between Israel and Egypt marked a significant breakthrough in the conflict. Under the guidance of United States President Jimmy Carter, the agreement normalized relations between the two countries and paved the way for further negotiations.

Throughout the conflict, terrorism and guerrilla warfare have played a destructive role. Palestinian nationalist groups, such as the Palestine Liberation Organization (PLO), employed these tactics to gain attention and leverage for their cause. The impact of these actions on the conflict cannot be underestimated and has further complicated peace efforts.

In conclusion, post-war peace efforts and United Nations resolutions have played a critical role in shaping the Arab-Israeli conflict. From the impact of British colonialism to the influence of external powers, the conflict remains complex and multifaceted. As historians, it is essential to analyze these historical events and developments to gain a comprehensive understanding of the Arab-Israeli conflict and its enduring consequences.

Chapter 9: The Role of International Organizations in Resolving the Arab-Israeli Conflict

United Nations' Involvement and Resolutions

The United Nations has played a significant role in the Arab-Israeli conflict, attempting to mediate and resolve the ongoing disputes between the parties involved. Since its establishment in 1945, the UN has been actively engaged in addressing the complex issues surrounding this conflict, reflecting the international community's recognition of its importance.

One of the earliest and most notable UN resolutions regarding the Arab-Israeli conflict was the 1947 UN Partition Plan, which proposed the division of Palestine into separate Jewish and Arab states. While the plan was accepted by the Jewish leadership, the Arab states rejected it, leading to the outbreak of violence and the subsequent 1948 Arab-Israeli War.

Over the years, the United Nations has passed numerous resolutions calling for peace, the protection of human rights, and the establishment of a Palestinian state. Resolution 242, passed in 1967 after the Six-Day War, called for the withdrawal of Israeli forces from territories occupied during the conflict and recognized the right of all states in the region to live in peace within secure and recognized boundaries.

However, the implementation of these resolutions has proven challenging, with both sides often failing to comply fully. The UN continues to face difficulties in enforcing its resolutions due to the complex nature of the conflict, deep-rooted historical grievances, and the influence of external powers.

The United Nations has also been actively involved in peace negotiations between Israel and its Arab neighbors. The Camp David Accords of 1978, brokered by the United States but with the support and involvement of the UN, led to a peace treaty between Israel and Egypt, the first between Israel and an Arab state.

Despite its efforts, the United Nations has faced criticism for its perceived bias towards either side of the conflict. Some argue that the organization has not done enough to hold Israel accountable for its actions, while others believe that it has been too critical of Israel, undermining its legitimacy as a neutral mediator.

In conclusion, the United Nations has been a central player in the Arab-Israeli conflict, attempting to mediate and resolve the disputes between the parties involved. Its resolutions have outlined principles for peace and called for the establishment of a Palestinian state, but the complex nature of the conflict and the influence of external powers have made their implementation challenging. Despite criticism, the UN's involvement remains crucial in the pursuit of a just and lasting resolution to this long-standing conflict.

Arab League's Influence and Initiatives

The Arab League, an organization formed in 1945, has played a significant role in shaping the Arab-Israeli conflict. Composed of 22 member states, the League has aimed to safeguard the collective interests of Arab nations and promote unity among them. Throughout its history, the organization has undertaken various initiatives and exerted its influence to address the complexities of the conflict.

One of the Arab League's early initiatives was the formulation of the Arab Peace Initiative in 2002. This comprehensive proposal offered Israel recognition and normalized relations with Arab states in exchange for a complete withdrawal from occupied territories and the establishment of a Palestinian state with East Jerusalem as its capital. The initiative demonstrated the League's commitment to resolving the conflict through diplomatic means and provided a potential framework for a comprehensive peace agreement.

Another important role the Arab League has played is in supporting the Palestinian cause. The organization has consistently condemned Israeli policies and actions that violate Palestinian rights, such as the establishment of Israeli settlements in occupied territories. The League has also provided financial aid and political support to the Palestinian Authority, helping to sustain their aspirations for statehood and self-determination.

Furthermore, the Arab League has utilized its diplomatic power to rally international support for the Palestinian cause. It has actively engaged with international organizations, including the United Nations, to advocate for the rights of Palestinians and push for resolutions condemning Israeli actions. The League's influence within these international forums has been crucial in shaping the narrative surrounding the conflict and garnering international attention.

In addition to its diplomatic efforts, the Arab League has also utilized economic measures to exert pressure on Israel. Through initiatives such as the Arab Boycott, Arab states have sought to isolate Israel economically, discouraging trade and investment with the country. These economic measures have been employed as a means of leveraging Arab states' collective power to influence Israeli policies and advance the Palestinian cause.

While the Arab League's initiatives and influence have undoubtedly had an impact on the Arab-Israeli conflict, it is important to acknowledge the complexities and limitations of their efforts. The League's unity has often been tested due to differing national interests among member states, hindering their ability to present a unified front.

Additionally, external powers such as the United States and the Soviet Union have played a significant role in the conflict, often overshadowing the League's influence.

Nevertheless, the Arab League continues to play a crucial role in addressing the Arab-Israeli conflict. Its initiatives and influence have helped shape the discourse surrounding the conflict, mobilized international support for the Palestinian cause, and provided a platform for Arab nations to collectively address their grievances. As the conflict persists, the Arab League's role remains vital in advocating for a just and lasting resolution.

External Mediation and Peace Processes

External mediation and peace processes have played a crucial role in the long and complex history of the Arab-Israeli conflict. As historians of this conflict, it is imperative for us to understand the impact of external actors and their attempts to bring about peace in a region marred by religious, cultural, and territorial disputes.

One significant influence on the Arab-Israeli conflict was the role of British colonialism. The Balfour Declaration of 1917, which expressed British support for the establishment of a Jewish homeland in Palestine, laid the groundwork for future tensions. The British Mandate in Palestine further exacerbated the conflict, as they struggled to balance the competing demands of Jewish and Arab populations. Understanding the impact of British colonial policies is essential in comprehending the roots of the conflict.

External powers, such as the United States and the Soviet Union, also exerted their influence throughout the Arab-Israeli conflict. The superpowers often aligned themselves with one side or the other, providing military, economic, and diplomatic support. Their involvement, motivated by geopolitical interests, often hindered peace processes and further polarized the conflict.

Religious and cultural differences have also played a significant role in the Arab-Israeli conflict. The clash between Jewish and Arab national movements, each rooted in their respective religious and cultural identities, has intensified tensions and hindered reconciliation. Understanding the complexities of these differences is crucial in analyzing the conflict's dynamics and potential for resolution.

Peace processes mediated by international organizations, such as the United Nations and the Arab League, have aimed to resolve the Arab-Israeli conflict. The negotiations at Camp David and the subsequent signing of the Camp David Accords in 1978 marked a significant turning point. However, the impact of these peace agreements on the conflict remains a subject of debate among historians.

The Israeli settlement movement and territorial disputes have further complicated the conflict. The establishment and expansion of Israeli settlements in the occupied territories have been a major obstacle to peace, as they continue to impede the creation of a viable Palestinian state. The Six-Day War of 1967, which resulted in Israel's occupation of the West Bank, Gaza Strip, and other territories, significantly altered the political and territorial landscape and continues to shape the conflict to this day.

Lastly, the role of terrorism and guerrilla warfare cannot be ignored in the Arab-Israeli conflict. Acts of violence perpetrated by both sides have had a devastating impact on civilian populations and have further deepened mistrust and animosity.

In conclusion, external mediation and peace processes have been crucial in attempting to resolve the Arab-Israeli conflict. The impact of British colonialism, the influence of external powers, the role of religious and cultural differences, territorial disputes, and the role of international organizations, as well as the influence of terrorism and guerrilla warfare, have all shaped the trajectory of this multifaceted conflict. As historians, it is our duty to analyze and assess these factors to gain a comprehensive understanding of the Arab-Israeli conflict and the prospects for peace in the region.

Challenges and Failures in Conflict Resolution

In the complex and protracted history of the Arab-Israeli conflict, numerous challenges and failures have hindered the path towards a peaceful resolution. From the impact of British colonialism and the role of religious and cultural differences, to the influence of external powers and the rise of Palestinian nationalism, these factors have shaped the conflict and posed significant obstacles to its resolution.

The impact of British colonialism on the Arab-Israeli conflict cannot be understated. The Balfour Declaration of 1917, which expressed British support for a Jewish homeland in Palestine, set the stage for decades of tension and conflict between Jewish settlers and the indigenous Arab population. The British Mandate period witnessed growing resentment from both sides, as the establishment of a Jewish state clashed with the aspirations of Arab nationalism. This legacy of colonialism continues to shape the conflict to this day.

Religious and cultural differences have also played a central role in perpetuating the Arab-Israeli conflict. The competing claims to the land of Palestine by Jews and Arabs, rooted in religious and historical narratives, have fueled a deep-seated animosity. The holy sites of Jerusalem, including the Al-Aqsa Mosque and the Western Wall, are at the heart of this issue, further exacerbating tensions and making compromise difficult.

External powers, particularly the United States and the Soviet Union, have exerted significant influence on the Arab-Israeli conflict. Cold War dynamics and geopolitical interests often overshadowed the pursuit of peace, as these superpowers supported their respective allies and perpetuated the conflict through arms sales and political maneuvering.

Palestinian nationalism emerged as a powerful force in the late 20th century, further complicating efforts to resolve the conflict. The Palestinian Liberation Organization (PLO) and its leader Yasser Arafat sought to establish an independent Palestinian state, leading to violent confrontations with Israel. The failure to address the aspirations of Palestinian nationalism has been a major stumbling block in the peace process.

The Israeli settlement movement, characterized by the establishment of Jewish communities in the occupied territories, has significantly impacted the Arab-Israeli conflict. The expansion of settlements has led to territorial disputes and border conflicts, further entrenching divisions and undermining the prospects for a two-state solution.

The Six-Day War of 1967 had a profound impact on the Arab-Israeli conflict. Israel's swift victory and subsequent occupation of the West Bank and Gaza Strip intensified the conflict, creating new challenges and grievances that persist to this day.

International organizations, such as the United Nations and the Arab League, have played a role in attempts to resolve the conflict. However, their efforts have often been stymied by political divisions and the veto power of major powers, limiting their effectiveness.

The Camp David Accords of 1978 marked a significant milestone in the peace process, as Israel and Egypt signed a peace treaty. However, the accords failed to address the core issues of the conflict, such as the status of Jerusalem and the rights of the Palestinian people, leaving the conflict unresolved.

Terrorism and guerrilla warfare have also had a profound impact on the Arab-Israeli conflict. From the rise of groups like Hamas and Hezbollah to acts of violence committed by both sides, terrorism has further deepened mistrust and hindered efforts towards reconciliation.

In conclusion, the Arab-Israeli conflict has faced numerous challenges and failures in its pursuit of resolution. From the impact of British colonialism and religious differences to the influence of external powers and the rise of Palestinian nationalism, these factors have shaped the conflict and impeded its resolution. The Israeli settlement movement, territorial disputes, and the impact of the Six-Day War have further complicated the path to peace. Meanwhile, the role of international organizations, the Camp David Accords, and the influence of terrorism and guerrilla warfare have all had significant implications. Understanding these challenges and failures is essential for historians seeking to unravel the complexities of the Arab-Israeli conflict and analyze its ongoing impact on the region.

Chapter 10: The Impact of the Camp David Accords on the Arab-Israeli Conflict

Background and Negotiation Process

The Arab-Israeli conflict is a complex and multifaceted struggle that has spanned decades, with roots deeply embedded in history, religion, and politics. Understanding the background and negotiation process of this conflict is crucial for historians seeking to analyze its causes, dynamics, and potential solutions.

The conflict can be traced back to the early 20th century when the British Empire issued the Balfour Declaration in 1917. This declaration expressed support for the establishment of a Jewish homeland in Palestine, an act that had significant consequences for the Arab-Israeli conflict. It laid the groundwork for the Zionist movement and the subsequent influx of Jewish immigrants to Palestine, which fueled tensions between Jewish settlers and the Arab population.

British colonialism played a pivotal role in shaping the Arab-Israeli conflict. The mandate period, from 1920 to 1948, witnessed British control over Palestine and the implementation of policies that favored Jewish immigration and settlement. These policies further exacerbated tensions between Jews and Arabs, setting the stage for future conflicts.

Religious and cultural differences have also played a significant role in the Arab-Israeli conflict. The land of Palestine holds immense religious significance for Jews, Muslims, and Christians, making it a focal point of contention. Jerusalem, in particular, has been a flashpoint due to its religious significance to all three faiths. These differences have fueled religious and cultural nationalism, contributing to the depth and complexity of the conflict.

External powers, such as the United States and the Soviet Union, have exerted considerable influence on the Arab-Israeli conflict. The United States, in particular, has been a major supporter of Israel, providing military aid and political backing. The Soviet Union, on the other hand, aligned itself with Arab states, contributing to the arms race and further fueling tensions in the region.

The role of Palestinian nationalism cannot be understated in the Arab-Israeli conflict. The Palestinian people have struggled for self-determination and statehood, leading to the rise of various nationalist movements. These movements, such as the Palestine Liberation Organization (PLO), have been central players in negotiation processes aimed at resolving the conflict.

Territorial disputes and border conflicts have been persistent issues in the Arab-Israeli conflict. The establishment of the State of Israel in 1948 resulted in the displacement of hundreds of thousands of Palestinians, leading to claims over land and boundaries. The Six-Day War in 1967 further intensified these disputes, with Israel gaining control over the West Bank, Gaza Strip, and other territories.

International organizations, including the United Nations and the Arab League, have played a role in attempting to resolve the Arab-Israeli conflict. The United Nations partition plan in 1947 aimed to create separate Jewish and Arab states, but was met with resistance and ultimately resulted in war. The Camp David Accords in 1978 brought about peace between Egypt and Israel but did not fully resolve the wider conflict.

The influence of terrorism and guerrilla warfare has also had a profound impact on the Arab-Israeli conflict. Groups like Hamas and Hezbollah have employed tactics such as suicide bombings and rocket attacks, leading to cycles of violence and retaliation.

In conclusion, understanding the background and negotiation process of the Arab-Israeli conflict is crucial for historians studying this complex and enduring struggle. Factors such as British colonialism, religious and cultural differences, external powers, Palestinian nationalism, territorial disputes, and the role of international organizations and terrorism have all shaped the conflict, making it a rich and multifaceted subject of historical analysis.

Egypt-Israel Peace Treaty and Regional Implications

The Egypt-Israel Peace Treaty signed in 1979 marked a significant turning point in the history of the Arab-Israeli conflict. This subchapter explores the regional implications of this historic agreement and its impact on various aspects of the conflict.

The peace treaty between Egypt and Israel was a result of the Camp David Accords, brokered by U.S. President Jimmy Carter. The agreement marked the first time an Arab country recognized Israel's right to exist and established diplomatic relations. The treaty not only ended decades of hostility between Egypt and Israel but also had far-reaching implications for the wider region.

One of the most significant regional implications of the peace treaty was the erosion of Arab unity against Israel. Egypt, being the most populous and influential Arab state, had played a leading role in the Arab-Israeli conflict. Its decision to make peace with Israel strained relations with other Arab nations and weakened the collective Arab stance against Israel. This fragmentation of Arab unity had a profound impact on the dynamics of the conflict.

Moreover, the peace treaty opened avenues for increased cooperation and normalization between Israel and other Arab states. Although many Arab nations initially condemned Egypt's decision, the treaty paved the way for later peace agreements, such as the Jordan-Israel peace treaty in 1994 and the Abraham Accords signed between Israel and the United Arab Emirates and Bahrain in 2020. The Egypt-Israel Peace Treaty thus set a precedent for future diplomatic engagements and regional cooperation.

Furthermore, the peace treaty had significant implications for the Palestinian cause. Egypt had been a key supporter of Palestinian nationalism, and its withdrawal from the conflict created a power vacuum in the Arab world. The treaty did include provisions for Palestinian self-rule, but its impact on the overall Palestinian struggle remains a topic of debate and controversy. Some argue that it weakened the Palestinian cause, while others believe it provided an opportunity for the Palestinians to negotiate a peaceful resolution.

The Egypt-Israel Peace Treaty also demonstrated the influence of external powers on the Arab-Israeli conflict. The United States played a pivotal role in brokering the peace agreement, highlighting its power and influence in the region. The Soviet Union, too, had a stake in the conflict and its influence waned with the signing of the peace treaty. The involvement of these superpowers underscored the geopolitical dimensions of the conflict.

In conclusion, the Egypt-Israel Peace Treaty had significant regional implications, ranging from the fragmentation of Arab unity to the normalization of relations between Israel and other Arab states. Its impact on the Palestinian cause, the influence of external powers, and the changing dynamics of the conflict are all crucial aspects to consider when analyzing the history of the Arab-Israeli conflict. Understanding the implications of this treaty is vital for historians studying the complexities and intricacies of this enduring conflict.

Palestinian Autonomy and Self-Governance

Palestinian autonomy and self-governance have been central issues in the Arab-Israeli conflict, with significant implications for the history of the conflict. This subchapter will explore the various aspects related to the Palestinian quest for self-rule and its impact on the conflict, shedding light on the role of external powers, the influence of religious and cultural differences, territorial disputes, and the impact of key events such as the Six-Day War and the Camp David Accords.

One of the fundamental factors that have shaped the Palestinian struggle for autonomy is the impact of British colonialism. The British Mandate over Palestine, established after World War I and lasting until 1948, set the stage for the conflict by facilitating Jewish immigration and the establishment of Zionist settlements, while simultaneously promising Arab self-determination. This contradiction sowed the seeds of tension and led to a deep sense of betrayal among Palestinians.

Religious and cultural differences have also played a significant role in the conflict. The Arab-Israeli conflict is deeply intertwined with the Israeli-Palestinian conflict, which has a strong nationalistic and religious component. The role of Palestinian nationalism and the desire for self-determination cannot be underestimated, as it has been a driving force for Palestinians in their struggle against Israeli control.

External powers, such as the United States and the Soviet Union, have exerted considerable influence on the Arab-Israeli conflict. These global powers have often supported one side over the other, shaping the dynamics of the conflict and hindering or facilitating the prospects for Palestinian autonomy. The United States, in particular, has played a crucial role as a mediator, especially during key events such as the Camp David Accords.

Territorial disputes and border conflicts have been at the core of the Arab-Israeli conflict. The establishment of Israeli settlements in the occupied territories has been a significant obstacle to Palestinian self-governance, as it has led to the dispossession of Palestinians from their land and the fragmentation of their communities. The impact of the Six-Day War in 1967 further exacerbated these territorial disputes, with Israel occupying the West Bank, Gaza Strip, and East Jerusalem.

International organizations, including the United Nations and the Arab League, have played a role in attempting to resolve the Arab-Israeli conflict. These organizations have proposed various resolutions and initiatives aimed at achieving a peaceful resolution and facilitating Palestinian autonomy. The Camp David Accords, signed between Israel and Egypt in 1978, represented a significant milestone in the conflict, as it marked the first Arab recognition of Israel's right to exist and paved the way for future peace negotiations.

Lastly, the influence of terrorism and guerrilla warfare cannot be overlooked in the context of the Arab-Israeli conflict. Palestinian militant groups, such as Hamas and the Palestine Liberation Organization (PLO), have employed these tactics in their struggle for self-governance, often targeting Israeli civilians. These acts of violence have further complicated the conflict and hindered the prospects for a peaceful resolution.

In conclusion, the issue of Palestinian autonomy and self-governance has been a central aspect of the Arab-Israeli conflict. Understanding the historical context, the impact of external powers, religious and cultural differences, territorial disputes, and key events such as the Six-Day War and the Camp David Accords is crucial to comprehending the complexities of this conflict and its potential for resolution.

Legacy and Unresolved Issues

The Arab-Israeli conflict has left a lasting legacy of unresolved issues that continue to shape the region's political landscape. This subchapter delves into the various aspects that have contributed to the perpetuation of this conflict and explores the impact they have had on its course.

One of the key factors that have influenced the Arab-Israeli conflict is the legacy of British colonialism. The British played a significant role in shaping the political and territorial landscape of the region through the Balfour Declaration of 1917, which expressed support for the establishment of a Jewish homeland in Palestine. This declaration laid the foundation for the ongoing conflict and created a sense of mistrust and resentment among the Arab population.

Religious and cultural differences have also played a crucial role in fueling the conflict. The clash between Judaism and Islam, as well as the competing claims to the holy city of Jerusalem, have deepened the divisions and made finding a resolution more challenging.

External powers, such as the United States and the Soviet Union, have exerted their influence on the Arab-Israeli conflict. These superpowers have often pursued their own interests, further complicating the resolution of the conflict and contributing to its protraction.

Palestinian nationalism has emerged as a powerful force in the Arab-Israeli conflict. The Palestinian people's quest for self-determination and statehood has been a central issue, and their struggle for national identity has fueled the conflict.

The Israeli settlement movement has had a significant impact on the Arab-Israeli conflict. The establishment and expansion of Israeli settlements in the occupied territories have been a major source of contention and have hindered the prospects of a peaceful resolution.

Territorial disputes and border conflicts have been a recurring theme in the Arab-Israeli conflict. The competing claims to land and the establishment of secure borders have been major obstacles to reaching a lasting peace agreement.

The Six-Day War of 1967 had a profound impact on the Arab-Israeli conflict. Israel's stunning military victory and subsequent occupation of the West Bank, Gaza Strip, and other territories further complicated the conflict and sparked Palestinian resistance.

International organizations, such as the United Nations and the Arab League, have played a role in attempting to resolve the Arab-Israeli conflict. However, their efforts have often been undermined by the deep-rooted divisions and conflicting interests of the parties involved.

The Camp David Accords of 1978 marked a significant milestone in the Arab-Israeli conflict. The peace agreement between Egypt and Israel demonstrated the potential for peaceful resolution, but it also exposed the challenges of achieving a comprehensive solution involving all parties.

Finally, terrorism and guerrilla warfare have had a profound influence on the Arab-Israeli conflict. Non-state actors, such as Hamas and Hezbollah, have resorted to violence in their struggle against Israel, perpetuating the cycle of violence and making peace elusive.

In conclusion, the legacy and unresolved issues of the Arab-Israeli conflict are deeply rooted in the complex interplay of historical, political, religious, and cultural factors. Understanding these dynamics is crucial for historians studying the conflict and for finding a path to a just and lasting peace in the region.

Chapter 11: The Influence of Terrorism and Guerrilla Warfare in the Arab-Israeli Conflict

Rise of Palestinian Militant Groups

The rise of Palestinian militant groups has been a significant aspect of the Arab-Israeli conflict, with profound implications for the region's history. This subchapter delves into the origins and development of these groups, examining their ideologies, strategies, and impact on the conflict.

The emergence of Palestinian militant groups can be traced back to the early 20th century when Palestinian nationalism started to take shape. Under British colonial rule, Palestinian Arabs experienced growing frustration and resentment towards Jewish immigration and the establishment of a Jewish homeland in Palestine. This discontent laid the foundation for the rise of Palestinian militant groups.

In the aftermath of the 1948 Arab-Israeli War and the creation of the state of Israel, displaced Palestinians sought to regain their lost homeland. This desire for self-determination led to the formation of various organizations, such as Fatah, the Popular Front for the Liberation of Palestine (PFLP), and Hamas. These groups employed different strategies, ranging from guerrilla warfare to acts of terrorism, in their struggle against Israel.

Religious and cultural differences played a crucial role in shaping the ideologies of these groups. While some were driven by secular nationalist ideals, others fused nationalism with Islamic fundamentalism. This blend of religion and nationalism gave rise to a new wave of militancy, with groups like Hamas advocating for the establishment of an Islamic state in Palestine.

External powers, such as the United States and the Soviet Union, also exerted influence on the conflict by providing military and financial support to various Palestinian factions. This external involvement further fueled the rise of militant groups and intensified the Arab-Israeli conflict.

The impact of Palestinian nationalism on the conflict cannot be overlooked. It has mobilized the Palestinian population and fostered a sense of unity and resistance against Israeli occupation. Additionally, the Israeli settlement movement, which aimed to establish Jewish settlements in the occupied territories, has been a major source of contention, leading to increased radicalization among Palestinians.

Territorial disputes and border conflicts have been a recurring theme in the Arab-Israeli conflict, and Palestinian militant groups have played a significant role in these conflicts. The Six-Day War in 1967, in which Israel gained control over the West Bank, Gaza Strip, and East Jerusalem, had a profound impact on the conflict and further galvanized the Palestinian resistance movement.

International organizations, such as the United Nations and the Arab League, have tried to mediate and resolve the conflict, but their efforts have often been hindered by the complexities and deep-rooted grievances on both sides. The Camp David Accords, signed in 1978 between Israel and Egypt, marked a significant milestone in the peace process, but the conflict has persisted, with intermittent waves of violence and terrorism.

In conclusion, the rise of Palestinian militant groups has been a central aspect of the Arab-Israeli conflict. Understanding the historical, cultural, and geopolitical factors behind their emergence is crucial for historians studying the conflict. Only by comprehending the complex dynamics at play can we hope to find a peaceful and just resolution to this long-standing dispute.

Suicide Bombings and Intensification of Violence

In the complex and protracted history of the Arab-Israeli conflict, suicide bombings have emerged as a harrowing and impactful tactic employed by various groups, intensifying violence and perpetuating a cycle of vengeance. This subchapter delves into the origins, motivations, and consequences of suicide bombings throughout the conflict, shedding light on their significant impact.

Suicide bombings, as a method of warfare, gained prominence in the late 20th century, particularly during the second intifada. Palestinian militant groups, such as Hamas and Islamic Jihad, utilized suicide bombings as a means to strike fear into Israeli society and exert pressure on the Israeli government. These attacks took place in civilian areas, inflicting a heavy toll on innocent lives and exacerbating the already volatile situation.

Religious and cultural differences played a crucial role in the emergence and justification of suicide bombings. The conflict between Israelis and Palestinians is deeply rooted in religious and nationalistic sentiments, with both sides claiming historical and religious ties to the land. Extremist interpretations of Islam, combined with a sense of desperation and hopelessness, have driven some individuals to believe that sacrificing their lives in a suicide bombing is a noble act that guarantees martyrdom and eternal salvation.

The influence of external powers on the Arab-Israeli conflict has also played a significant role in the rise of suicide bombings. The support provided by external actors, such as the United States and the Soviet Union during the Cold War era, has fueled the conflict by providing arms, funding, and political backing to different factions. These external powers have often pursued their own interests, further complicating the resolution of the conflict and perpetuating violence.

Suicide bombings have had far-reaching consequences, not only in terms of loss of life but also in shaping the trajectory of the conflict. The Israeli government responded to these attacks with increased security measures and military operations, leading to further resentment and radicalization among Palestinians. Moreover, suicide bombings have eroded trust and deepened the divide between Israelis and Palestinians, making it increasingly challenging to achieve a lasting peace.

Understanding the origins and impact of suicide bombings in the Arab-Israeli conflict is crucial for historians to grasp the complexities and dynamics of this enduring conflict. By examining the role of religious and cultural differences, external powers, and the consequences of these attacks, historians can contribute to a more comprehensive understanding of the conflict and potentially pave the way for a more nuanced approach to its resolution.

Israeli Counterterrorism Measures

In the tumultuous history of the Arab-Israeli conflict, the Israeli government has faced numerous challenges in combating terrorism and ensuring the safety and security of its citizens. This subchapter explores the various counterterrorism measures implemented by Israel over the years, shedding light on their effectiveness and impact on the conflict.

From its inception as a nation in 1948, Israel has been confronted with relentless acts of terrorism perpetrated by various groups seeking to undermine its existence. In response, the Israeli government has adopted a multifaceted approach to counterterrorism. This approach combines intelligence gathering, military operations, border security, and legal measures to thwart terrorist activities.

The Israeli intelligence community, renowned for its efficiency and effectiveness, plays a pivotal role in identifying and neutralizing potential threats. Mossad, Shin Bet, and Military Intelligence are the key agencies responsible for gathering intelligence, conducting surveillance, and infiltrating terrorist networks. Through their efforts, Israel has been able to prevent numerous attacks and dismantle terrorist cells.

The Israeli Defense Forces (IDF) have also been at the forefront of counterterrorism operations. They employ a range of tactics, including targeted assassinations, airstrikes, and ground incursions, to eliminate high-value targets and disrupt terrorist activities. While these military operations have been criticized for their impact on civilian populations, they have undoubtedly weakened the capabilities of terrorist organizations.

Border security has been another crucial aspect of Israel's counterterrorism strategy. The construction of barriers, such as the West Bank barrier and the Gaza border fence, has significantly reduced the infiltration of terrorists into Israeli territory. These physical barriers, coupled with advanced surveillance technologies, have proven effective in thwarting terrorist attacks.

Additionally, Israel has implemented stringent legal measures to combat terrorism. The arrest and prosecution of individuals involved in terrorist activities, along with the demolition of the homes of terrorists, serve as deterrents and send a clear message that terrorism will not be tolerated.

Despite these measures, terrorism remains a persistent challenge in the Arab-Israeli conflict. The complex nature of the conflict, fueled by religious and cultural differences, external powers, and territorial disputes, poses unique challenges for Israeli counterterrorism efforts. Nevertheless, Israel's robust and comprehensive approach to counterterrorism has undoubtedly saved countless lives and contributed to the overall security of the nation.

As historians analyze the Arab-Israeli conflict, it is crucial to examine the impact of Israeli counterterrorism measures on the course of events. Understanding the successes and limitations of these measures can provide valuable insights into the broader dynamics of the conflict and the complexities of addressing terrorism in a protracted conflict.

International Responses and Efforts to Combat Terrorism

In the complex and protracted history of the Arab-Israeli conflict, terrorism and guerrilla warfare have played a significant role. Both sides have employed these tactics to further their respective causes, resulting in widespread violence, loss of life, and political turmoil. However, the international community has not remained passive in the face of such challenges, and various responses and efforts have been made to combat terrorism and bring about a resolution to the conflict.

One of the key players in this regard has been the United Nations (UN). The UN has consistently condemned acts of terrorism and called for peaceful negotiations and dialogue to resolve the Arab-Israeli conflict. It has sponsored numerous resolutions, initiatives, and peacekeeping missions aimed at deescalating tensions and fostering a peaceful resolution between the parties involved. However, the effectiveness of these efforts has been hindered by political divisions and the veto power of the Security Council's permanent members, particularly the United States and the Soviet Union during the Cold War.

Another important international organization involved in resolving the conflict is the Arab League. Comprising of Arab nations, the Arab League has advocated for the rights of the Palestinian people and sought to address their grievances by supporting their cause diplomatically and financially. However, internal divisions and conflicting interests among member states have often hampered the

Arab League's ability to present a united front and achieve meaningful progress in resolving the conflict.

External powers, such as the United States and the Soviet Union, have also exerted their influence in the Arab-Israeli conflict. The United States, in particular, has played a prominent role, often aligning itself with Israel and providing military and financial aid. This support has been a source of contention, as some argue that it has perpetuated the conflict and hindered efforts towards a just and lasting peace. The Soviet Union, on the other hand, supported Arab nations and Palestinian liberation movements, contributing to the overall complexity of the conflict.

Efforts to combat terrorism and bring about a resolution to the Arab-Israeli conflict have also involved diplomatic initiatives and peace agreements. The Camp David Accords, signed in 1978 between Israel and Egypt, marked a significant step towards peace in the region. Under this agreement, Israel agreed to return the Sinai Peninsula to Egypt, and both parties committed to resolving their differences through peaceful means. Despite its limitations and the subsequent challenges faced in implementing its provisions, the Camp David Accords demonstrated the potential for peaceful negotiations to yield tangible results.

In conclusion, the Arab-Israeli conflict has witnessed various international responses and efforts to combat terrorism and foster peace. Organizations such as the UN and the Arab League, as well as external powers like the United States and the Soviet Union, have all played significant roles in attempting to bring about a resolution. However, the complex nature of the conflict, coupled with political divisions and conflicting interests, have often hindered progress towards a just and lasting peace. Nonetheless, diplomatic initiatives and peace agreements, such as the Camp David Accords, have demonstrated the potential for peaceful negotiations to yield positive outcomes in the quest for a resolution to the conflict.